LA

AlFREDO

CHANGO
FOC

— JOAQUIN THE MA

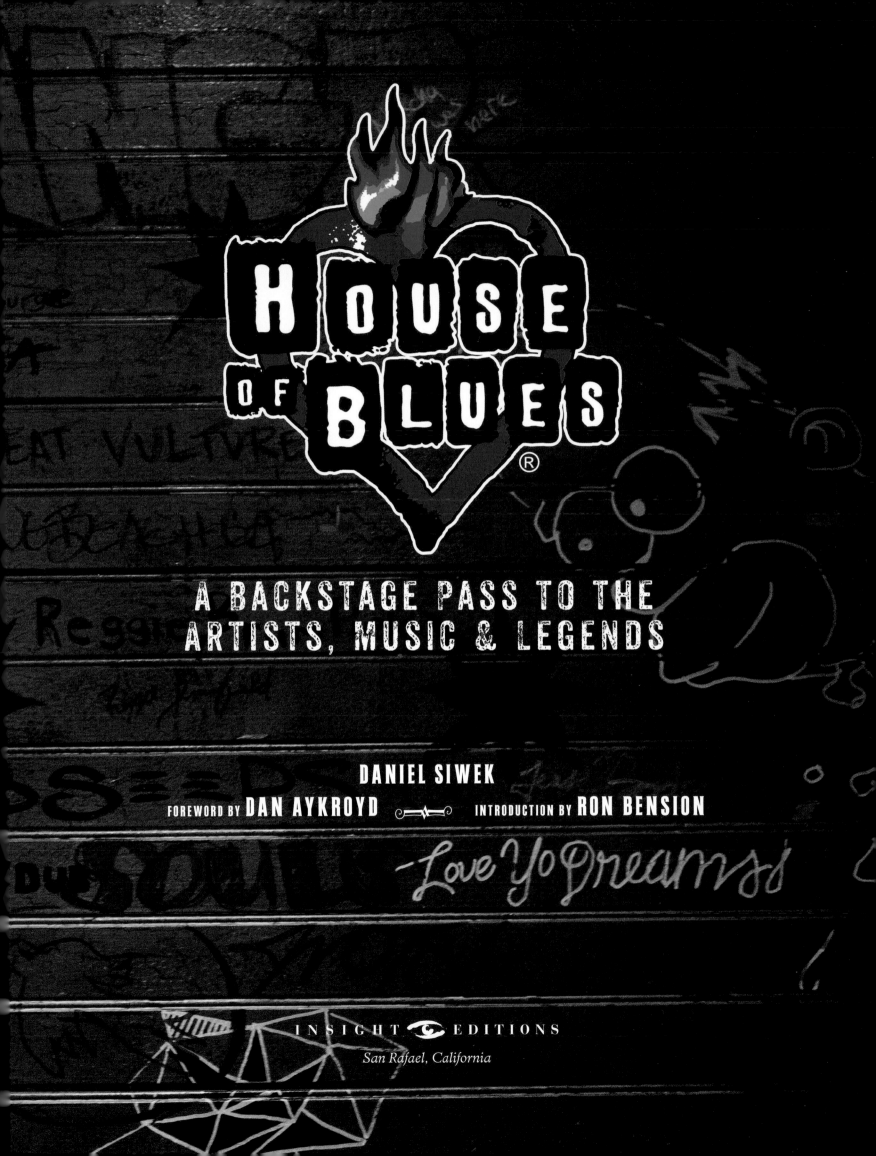

HOUSE OF BLUES

A BACKSTAGE PASS TO THE ARTISTS, MUSIC & LEGENDS

DANIEL SIWEK

FOREWORD BY **DAN AYKROYD** ⟶ INTRODUCTION BY **RON BENSION**

INSIGHT ◉ EDITIONS

San Rafael, California

INSIGHT
EDITIONS

PO Box 3088
San Rafael, CA 94912
www.insighteditions.com

www.INSIGHTEDITIONS.com

FOR WEB EXCLUSIVE CONTENT!

Find us on Facebook: www.facebook.com/InsightEditions
Follow us on Twitter: @insighteditions

Library of Congress Cataloging-in-Publication Data available.

ISBN: 978-1-60887-253-4

ROOTS of PEACE   REPLANTED PAPER

Insight Editions, in association with Roots of Peace, will plant two
trees for each tree used in the manufacturing of this book. Roots
of Peace is an internationally renowned humanitarian organization
dedicated to eradicating land mines worldwide and converting
war-torn lands into productive farms and wildlife habitats. Roots
of Peace will plant two million fruit and nut trees in Afghanistan
and provide farmers there with the skills and support necessary for
sustainable land use.

Manufactured in Hong Kong by Insight Editions

10 9 8 7 6 5 4 3 2 1

CONTENTS

FOREWORD

HOUSE OF BLUES would not exist if it weren't for the passion and vision of third-generation master entrepreneur Isaac Tigrett. In 1992, this entertainment innovator approached Judy Belushi and me with the idea of reviving the legend of Jake and Elwood, nurturing that legend as a brand, and using it to provide artists and audiences with premium, technologically advanced, visually impactful, and all-around-fun juke joints.

Through his intimate knowledge of Southern culture, music, architecture, and cuisine, Tigrett curated a rich, authentic experience by bringing rural folk art to House of Blues walls and Louisiana cooking to its kitchens. In fact, House of Blues has one of the most valuable folk art collections on the planet and features seriously renowned and celebrated talents such as Howard Finster, Roy Ferdinand, Leroy Almon, Jimmy Lee Sudduth, and John Bok. At each of our thirteen venues you can sit and look at some of the world's finest folk art and enjoy New Orleans–style jambalaya before taking a seat at one of the rail tables in the showrooms to see artists ranging from B.B. King and Bob Dylan to John Legend and Jay-Z.

House of Blues is a house of all music. Our nightclubs are recognized by audiences and performers alike as unparalleled places to create incredible memories with their favorite artists. With this book, I invite you to take a journey through twenty years of amazing moments and explore the sights, sounds, and tastes of the one-of-a-kind experience I have been proud to be a part of—the place where I have performed with the legendary Blues Brothers band many, many times—and my favorite place to hang out: House of Blues.

Please enjoy this record of a concept that commands stimulation for all the senses.

—Dan Aykroyd, aka Elwood Blues

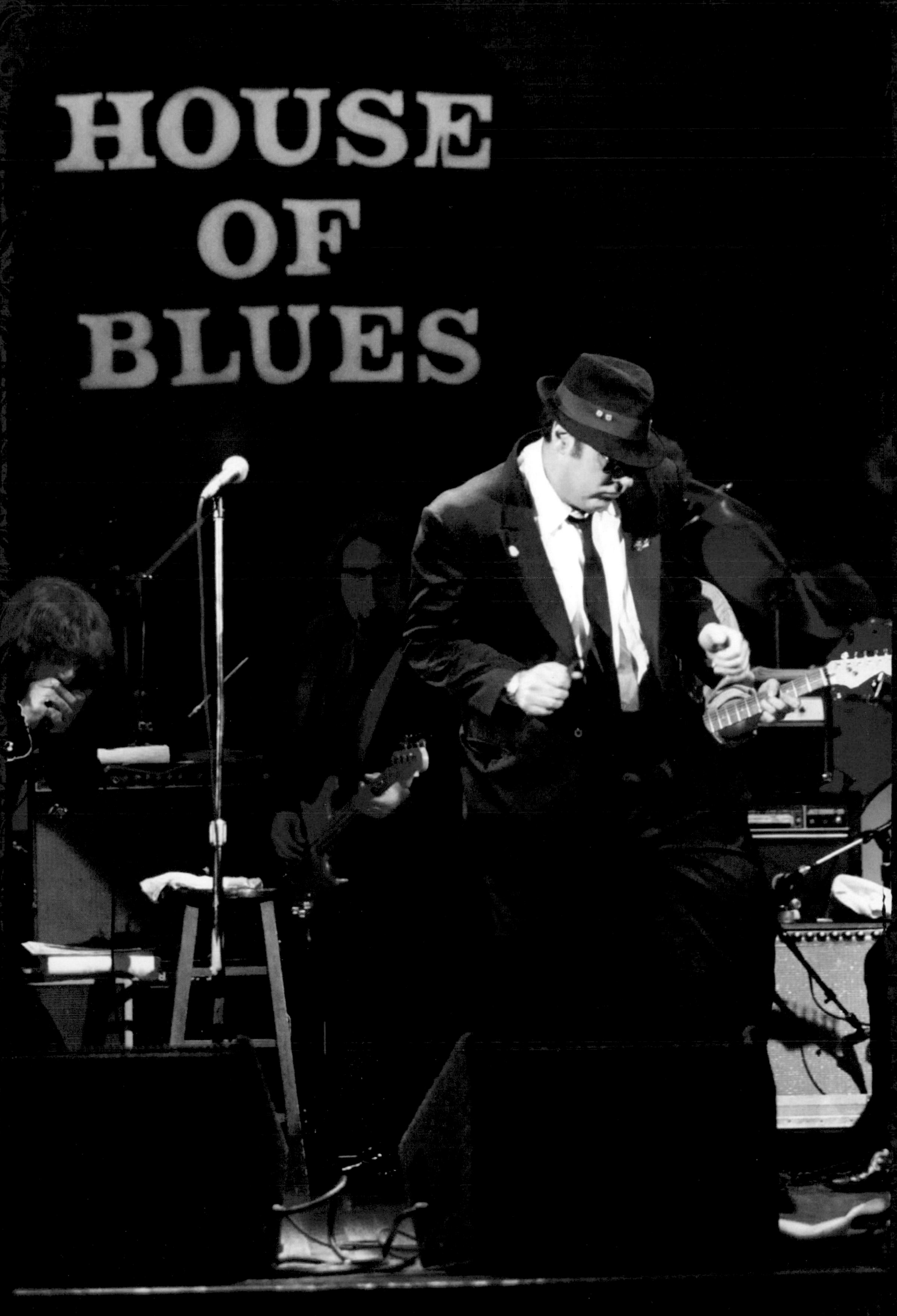
HOUSE
OF
BLUES

INTRODUCTION

AT HOUSE OF BLUES, our mission is simple: Create great experiences through live music. This has been the keynote of House of Blues since its humble beginnings in Cambridge, Massachusetts, where in 1992 a single, 220-capacity juke joint set a new precedent for live entertainment and helped revitalize that uniquely American musical form we call the blues. Just as blues music is the foundation for everything from soul and jazz to hip-hop and rock and roll, that little venue in Harvard Square was the seed from which a collective of iconic venues would eventually grow. Championing blues legends as well as emerging artists, House of Blues Cambridge celebrated the roots of modern American music even while looking to the future.

Today House of Blues is the largest collection of live entertainment clubs and theaters in the world. But, as Dan Aykroyd proudly points out, "the juke joint feeling of House of Blues has never dissipated, from our first tiny little club in Cambridge to our superflagship in Chicago." With thirteen soulfully stylized locations dedicated to superior sound and staging, our houses are the finest music venues anywhere, providing intimate live experiences for fans and musicians across the country.

Each is a home for emerging artists, and each is *the* place where established stars go to get up close and personal with the audience. But House of Blues is much more than a concert hall. The foundation is music, but the enduring goal is to provide extraordinary service, offer outstanding food, curate unique works of art, dish out good vibes, generate funds for the International House of Blues Foundation, and showcase musical talent through venues that refuse to compromise on quality.

House of Blues delivers the best band and fan experience in the industry. The intimacy of the venues, along with the proximity of the stage to the dance floor, creates an atmosphere where bands can connect with their fans. It is the celebration of this connection that is the heart of House of Blues and the crux of this collection of stories and images chronicling its history.

Just as blues music was conceived by folks who were eager to croon about the realities of the world they lived in—and who could do so with conviction because their feet were firmly on the ground—so too are the tales that make up *House of Blues: A Backstage Pass to the Artists, Music & Legends*. Like the stories that have played a part in the mythology of bluesmen like Robert Johnson, the legacy of House of Blues is best expressed through oral histories told by those who helped conceive and found what has become an entertainment institution, as well as those who have played House of Blues' stages, from Orlando to L.A.

Voices such as that of House of Blues founder Isaac Tigrett reveal the dedication to conceptual integrity behind every venue and the commitment to creating an establishment based on human values. Dan Aykroyd and Jim Belushi speak to the celebration of music, art, culture, and community that is the backbeat of every event hosted by House of Blues. Blues artists such as Bobby Rush and Shemekia Copeland talk of the renewed interest in blues music inspired by House of Blues, while other artists confess the pleasures of playing in a venue that takes care of the talent. And the many others who have been there since day one and privy to the backstage-story recall what are undoubtedly some of the most spectacular moments in music history.

In fact, since opening in 1992, House of Blues has hosted some of the greatest musical legends ever to walk onstage: Eric Clapton, the Who, Prince, Lady Gaga, B.B. King, Clarence "Gatemouth" Brown, Etta James, Tupac, Daft Punk, Billy Idol, ZZ Top, the Raspberries, James Brown . . . the list could go on and on. Committed to diverse booking and exalting the roots of it all, the blues, House of Blues stands above the rest as the premier venue to experience live music.

Stop by a House of Blues, and I promise we will bring you music that will feed your soul.

—*Ron Bension*

PAGE 7: Dan Aykroyd performing at HOB Chicago during John Belushi's birthday celebration.

OPPOSITE: Bo Diddley with his trademark rectangular guitar at HOB L.A. Bo Diddley was also known as the Originator for his role in shepherding the transition from blues to rock.

PAGES 10–11: Keb' Mo', known for his modern take on Delta blues, onstage at HOB L.A.

chapter one

CROSSROADS

There's a juke joint on the corner of Sunset Boulevard and Olive Drive in Los Angeles. It's not a nightclub or a café, not a ballroom or a bistro, not a bar or a grill, but a juke joint. There's another juke joint on the corner of East Third Street and Euclid Avenue in Cleveland, and another on Decatur Street in New Orleans. And we've got ten more that—no matter if situated inside a vintage coffee-processing plant in Dallas, an old pirate haunt in Myrtle Beach, an opera house in Chicago, or a casino in Las Vegas—are all juke joints. And all meet at one place . . . the crossroads: the crossroads of culture and cuisine, classroom and concert hall, outsider art and museum repertory, hedonism and humanitarianism, secularism and spiritualism, legend and reality, rhythm and blues, and, literally, *the* Crossroads of Highway 61 and Highway 49. Because it is there, in the deep Delta of Clarksdale, Mississippi, where our inspiration was sonically, conceptually, and, in one case, physically born.

They say the blues was born on Beale Street in Memphis, Tennessee, where, in 1900, W. C. Handy wrote "Memphis Blues," but it was the intersection of Highways 61 and 49 where ethnomusicologist Alan Lomax went in search of Robert Johnson. Lomax had heard a rumor about Robert Johnson, a rumor that had been spreading like wildfire, a rumor that Johnson—a mildly successful musician but nothing too hot—had knelt down at the Crossroads, prayed to anybody who would listen, and found an audience with the underworld. Robert Johnson offered to sell his soul to the devil for success. No one knows who signed the other side of that dotted line, but whether he called himself the Devil, Beelzebub, Mephistopheles, Legba, or Satan himself, it was a Faustian deal that Johnson couldn't refuse—one

that not only shined a light on his prowess but also blazed a trail for blues masters to follow.

By the time Lomax, carrying his recording equipment, arrived at the Stovall Plantation—a large property just a stone's throw from the Crossroads, with its own moonshine distillery and juke joint where sharecroppers could party and get down—Johnson was dead and gone. But, as luck would have it, he heard the picking of Muddy Waters coming from an old slave house nearby. Muddy's hero, Son House, was also there, and as these and other bluesmen took part in the Great Migration from the Delta to all points north, west, and east, they took their tunes with them. Eventually, the blues—a music that evolved from field chants and chain gang hymns alongside gospel—would be

OPPOSITE: Depiction of Robert Johnson by Josephine Wallis, on display at HOB San Diego.

performed in other juke joints, supper clubs, recording studios, and churches from coast to coast, and it would soon influence emerging genres like jazz, R&B, rock and roll, soul, and roots reggae and, eventually, hip-hop, hard rock, heavy metal, punk, and even techno and electronic dance music (EDM).

House of Blues commemorates the musical and cultural gifts received at the Crossroads by burying dirt from that fated intersection beneath the stage and entrance of every venue in a ceremony they call the "Mississippi Mud Pour." It may be out of sight, but it's never out of mind as it silently greets every guest and fortifies the foundation of every stage. And the "Crazy Quilt" stage curtains welcome all in a colorful pastiche that serves as a metaphor of how much stronger we are when the diverse fabrics of a community are stitched together. Just above the "Crazy Quilt" is the "God Wall" which features the religious symbols of all faiths and the phrase *ALL IS ONE*. That's because

no matter what god you celebrate or which style of music you've come to enjoy, at House of Blues it's "One Nation Under a Groove." And come Sunday, everyone shows up to testify at Gospel Brunch—where souls are served and the roots of blues music recalled in every hymn.

Welcome to our juke joint. The house has been rocking for twenty years strong, but don't worry, you didn't miss a thing, because there ain't no party like a House of Blues party, and this House of Blues party don't stop. Come with us now, behind the "Crazy Quilt," if you will. This book is your backstage pass, your all-access laminate, your glittery VIP wristband that invites you up to our Foundation Room, where you can kick back and hear the rest of the story—from Elwood Blues himself, Dan Aykroyd; the visionary who dreamed up House of Blues, Isaac Tigrett; the performers who leave it all on the stage at House of Blues; and the many movers and shakers behind House of Blues and its music, legends, and legacy.

HE'S A SOUL MAN: MEET DAN AYKROYD

Dan Aykroyd wears many hats, some cone shaped, others black wool felt fedoras. He is also famous for playing many roles: As Elwood Blues, he'll always be a Blues Brother, but anyone who can share the stage with Sam & Dave and James Brown is also a Soul Man. Not only was he the first to believe in the concept of House of Blues, but this Canadian ham was also its biggest booster, putting his money where his harmonica was as the second-largest investor. He is a blues expert, turning folks on to the original masters and providing proper context to all disciples who follow on House of Blues Radio Hour (now The Blues Mobile with Elwood Blues). He believes in House of Blues, from the top of his fedora to the very bottom of his Rubber Biscuit of a soul. Twenty years later, he still proselytizes the purity, the integrity, and the mission of House of Blues.

DAN AYKROYD: The juke joint feeling of House of Blues has never dissipated, from our first tiny little club in Cambridge to our superflagship in Chicago. When you sit there and you look at that art and you listen to the music and you hear a concert, and have dinner in the Crossroads restaurant, where you're eating comfort food inspired by the cooking of the Deep South, you're getting as close to a juke joint experience as you would if you were, say, in Clarksdale or driving through the Mississippi hill country. We took this concept of a higher, more sophisticated communal experience between the artist and the audience and brought in staff and personnel who were able to connect right away with the design of the place, and the mission of the place, which is to help ever and hurt never. Other venues, restaurants, and concert halls simply don't have that appeal and the positive awareness that House of Blues does.

OPPOSITE: Mural art by Scott Guion on display at HOB L.A.

RIGHT: Elwood Blues outside HOB L.A.

TOP RIGHT: HOB founder Isaac Tigrett (left) with Michael Grozier, then HOB general manager and currently executive vice president of theater and club operations for Live Nation.

TRAIN KEPT A-ROLLIN': MEET ISAAC TIGRETT

If Dan Aykroyd is the Pied Piper of concert halls and restaurants, Isaac Tigrett is the William Randolph Hearst, and House of Blues is his San Simeon—only there's thirteen of them. He's the visionary, the master builder, the insatiable perfectionist, the collector of culture, art, artifacts, people, and even auras. And they've all served him well in creating, or possibly re-creating (he'd already founded Hard Rock Café), his ultimate escape, his ultimate hope—the juke joint version of Charles Kane's "Rosebud." Despite being a wealthy, dirty blond, blue-eyed white boy, Tigrett spent much of his youth surrounded by African American friends on the family porch, where they'd gather to work, sing songs, and swap yarns.

ISAAC TIGRETT: I'm the namesake of Isaac Burton Tigrett. He was my great-uncle and actually raised my father as his son. He made his fortune betting on the dieselization of the railroads. My family was prominent in the South, one of the founding families of a little town called Jackson, Tennessee, about seventy miles from Memphis. I grew up on Tigrett Place, and I went to Isaac Burton Tigrett Middle School, where I was beaten every day. My parents were always traveling, and I had a black nanny named Drewcilla Tuggle. She was a graduate of Lane College, which was one of the first African American colleges built after the Civil War. I really feel that I'm part of

HELP EVER
HURT NEVER

the black community because the entire culture I grew up with was so loving and amazing. My grandmother's place had a massive screened back porch and kitchen, and about eight or nine African American workers also lived there. We shucked corn, snapped beans, and canned stuff up while they sang songs and told stories. The influence continued with gospel music in the black churches, which I attended with Drewcilla every other week. It was such a deeply spiritual experience. If you go to the AME [African Methodist Episcopal] church down south, you really understand it.

DAN AYKROYD: Isaac is a true son of the South, and he understands Southern culture. He understands African American culture. He was there in Memphis, he was there in Nashville, and he knew players like Eddie Floyd. He was there at the most seminal time in American music, which, to us, was the Stax/Volt movement.

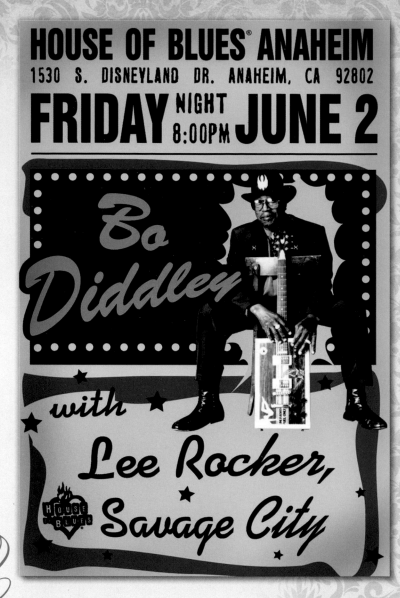

House of Blues poster: HOUSE OF BLUES® ANAHEIM 1530 S. Disneyland Dr. Anaheim, CA 92802 FRIDAY NIGHT 8:00PM JUNE 2 Bo Diddley with Lee Rocker, Savage City

> "BY THE TIME HE WAS SEVENTEEN, HE WAS ALREADY PROMOTING SHOWS AND HAD HIRED PEOPLE LIKE BOBBY BLAND AND BOBBY RUSH."
> —DAN AYKROYD

ISAAC TIGRETT: Otis Redding played my high school prom, and you had Sam & Dave, and Isaac Hayes, who became a dear and lifelong friend, and Booker T. & the MG's. They had Steve Cropper, Donald "Duck" Dunn, Lewis Steinberg, and Willie Hall, and they were considered the greatest rhythm section and the greatest innovators of that music. Rock and roll also started in Memphis, with Sam Phillips at Sun Records, which was the first time that white artists were doing black music. Phillips was the greatest rebel who ever existed in modern music. Howlin' Wolf was one

of the first to come out of that studio, and there was a lot of controversy around the idea of picking up on this black music—remember, this was the South. Sun Records also had Carl Perkins, the King of Rockabilly, who lived down the street from me and who I knew very well. Jerry Lee Lewis and Elvis came out of there as well. That was a little before my time. But when I was fifteen or sixteen we would go to Sun Records just for a kick. On a rainy day there would be eight hundred people standing out front for Elvis, and on a nice day there'd be two thousand.

DAN AYKROYD: Isaac went to see every black act that came through town, and he was a friend with all kinds of really wonderful, strong African American performers, writers, singers, photographers, and vocalists—he even drove Bo Diddley around. By the time he was seventeen, he was already promoting shows and had hired people like Bobby Bland and Bobby Rush.

OPPOSITE: Luther Allison performing at HOB Cambridge. Allison broke into the blues scene in 1957 when Howlin' Wolf invited him onstage.

Bobby Rush recorded alongside Bo Diddley at Chess Records, the label that brought you Willie Dixon, Muddy Waters, Little Walter, Chuck Berry, Howlin' Wolf, and many others. Like Tigrett, Rush gave rides, only he was lucky enough to chauffeur "At Last" star Etta James to the studio. He remembers playing a show or two for Tigrett back in the day and came back into the fold later at House of Blues.

BOBBY RUSH: Oh, yeah! Lord have mercy, Isaac goes way back with me, man! I remember that he came with some white schoolkids and tried to get me to play at his school. I was nervous because at that time James Brown also went to a white school to play and got booed. They wanted to throw him out because he was a black man, and so I was concerned—were they going to accept me, or were they going to do to me what they did to James Brown? But Isaac made me believe that it was a different day and a different time and that there wouldn't be those kinds of problems. And there weren't.

White youth of America helped advance the civil rights movement simply by singing and dancing and popularizing this predominantly black music, which was first known as "race music," then R&B, and then rock and roll, and soul. Elvis may have put a white face (or hips) on it, but in no time white girls were swooning over Little

Richard—*a black man in drag. As the social upheaval erupted in riots, the Cuban missile crisis, and the Vietnam War, so did the cultural explosion, which included the sexual revolution, the counterculture, and the British Invasion. The Brits didn't just bring their mop-tops. They regifted our own gospel backbeat and put a ribbon on our own underappreciated blues songs. Artists like Eric Clapton, Jeff Beck, the Rolling Stones, and Led Zeppelin used their sticky fingers to snag every blues lick they could find, basing their entire repertoires on unsung heroes like Willie Dixon, Muddy Waters, Howlin' Wolf, John Lee Hooker, and Elmore James. Even Jimi Hendrix, who introduced feedback to the national anthem, schooled us about Son House with the help of a British rhythm section.*

ISAAC TIGRETT: Then I went to England, where the scene was exploding. There was all this music that was influenced by the same culture I had just come from. I remember hanging out with Chris Jagger at his older brother Mick's house, known as Stargroves. It was this beautiful hundred-room house in the country, and we were sitting in this giant old kitchen in this ancient house in the summer of 1970, and they were listening to these old 78s of the early blues guys. It blew my mind to watch them grab a lick from this song, a phrase from that song, and create one of their best albums, *Sticky Fingers*.

TOP LEFT: Bobby Rush, day fishin'. Rush has more than twenty-five releases to his credit and a unique style that combines blues, soul, and funk.
BOTTOM RIGHT: Self-proclaimed Disciple of the Blues Sonny Rhodes feeling out a high note on his lap steel guitar at HOB Cambridge.

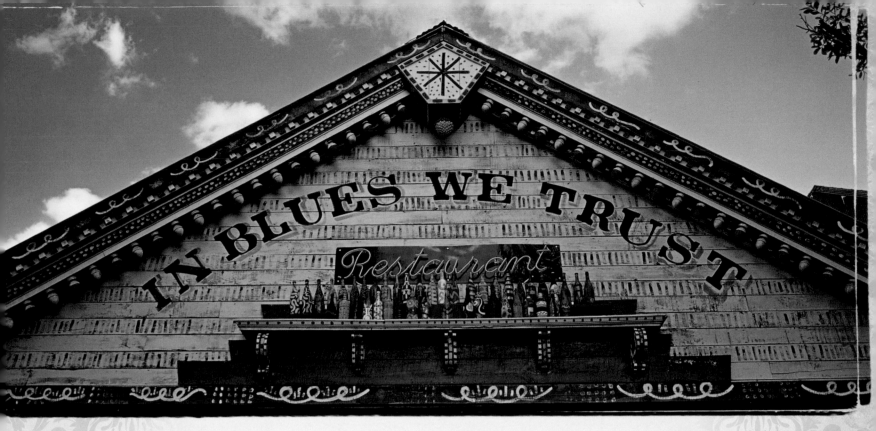

SAI BABA O'RILEY

Isaac Tigrett's travels found him in England, where he, along with countless musicians, was able to start his career on the wave of a great musical and cultural movement—rock and roll—and his Hard Rock Café was almost an instant success. But his spiritual journey had begun much earlier, when as a child he'd go with Drewcilla to the gospel churches in the South. And it continued through his adult life. Like many of his generation who had a religious experience when they turned on, tuned in, and dropped out, Tigrett sought alternatives to institutionalized religious practices. Lucy was in the sky with diamonds, all right, but she was also making the journey to India to hang out with Maharishi Mahesh Yogi, who offered a different kind of peace, love, and spiritual awakening through Transcendental Meditation. The Beatles helped introduce these Eastern practices to the pop culture of the time, and once Tigrett knew his business was stable enough for him to travel, he was sure to follow in their footsteps.

ISAAC TIGRETT: I put on a backpack and went to India for seven or eight months. I went to the Himalayas to find every guru and every yogi— and not just the ones who were alive, because the energies of the ones who had passed were just as powerful, at least to me. Then suddenly I met Sri Sathya Sai Baba, and the second I saw him I knew that he was the master teacher I was looking for.

Sai Baba told me, "I want you to start a business based on human values to show that you can have a business based on human values and still be successful." That's the message of House of Blues. I had the message before I had the business. Around that time I kept looking at what was going on in music. It was very interesting to me to watch the granddaddy of them all, blues music, become popular again. People are always looking for things that are real, things that have depth. And when I noticed how cities like Chicago, which started the blues explosion, were getting more than 500,000 visitors over two days for a blues festival, I saw the opportunity that I never thought I'd see in my lifetime again: taking a culture and putting an umbrella over it, creating an icon, creating a trademark that the marketplace relates to in terms of that culture.

But Isaac Tigrett had second thoughts about starting a new business, and before fully committing himself he went back to his guru, Sai Baba.

MICHAEL GROZIER: He said to Sai Baba, "Master, you know, they're asking me to get involved and do this club. I feel like I've already done it. I really don't want to do it again." And Sai Baba said back to him, "Hard Rock was high school. This is university."

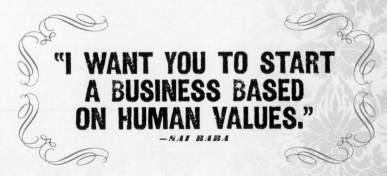

"I WANT YOU TO START A BUSINESS BASED ON HUMAN VALUES."
— *SAI BABA*

ABOVE: Facade of HOB New Orleans, boasting the club's keynote.

MEET THE BLUES BROTHERS

If Yankee Stadium is the holy house of its most revered players, then Dan Aykroyd and John Belushi, as Elwood and Jake, are the Lou Gehrig and Babe Ruth of House of Blues. The Blues Brothers couldn't help it—they were on a mission from God to revive the blues in a time when bloated arena rock and coked-up disco ruled the airwaves. What started out as a way for two buddies to blow off some steam in an after-hours bar ended up spilling over onto the stage of America's favorite late-night sketch comedy/variety shows, and eventually the silver screen, where the act became a pop culture phenomenon. They put a band together featuring most of those Stax Records guys they admired so much and made sure to acknowledge every cat who wrote the songs they were playing.

OPPOSITE: Vintage Jake and Elwood Blues (John Belushi and Dan Aykroyd, respectively) at home behind their Blues Brothers Bar, a speakeasy in Chicago's Old Town, which was shut down by authorities in 1982.

DAN AYKROYD: The Blues Brothers was a very honorable project. We weren't exploiting the music but rather paying tribute to the original artists who wrote the material. The money that Belushi and I got was from the album sales and the mechanical royalties for playing the harmonica and performing the vocals, but we did not get any publishing royalties because we were not the people who wrote the songs. They wrote the songs; they should benefit.

Michael Grozier, executive VP of clubs and theaters for Live Nation (parent company of House of Blues), played an invaluable role in the opening of House of Blues, and unlike many who lost their memories in a cloud of disco dust, he remembers the era well and recalls, too, the essential role the Blues Brothers played in the success of House of Blues.

MICHAEL GROZIER: People like James Brown, Aretha Franklin, and Ray Charles—they were already on the heap, right? The Blues Brothers was a renaissance for all those artists. If you think about it, the Blues Brothers movie came out at a time when cocaine was everywhere, especially in the club scene, and diet disco dominated the airwaves. But here's a bunch of guys in black suits and fedoras and dark sunglasses, and they brought John Lee Hooker forward, because he mattered, and Aretha Franklin, because she mattered. You could see that the love for blues music as an indigenous American art form was so deep in Dan, and ultimately became a passion for John, too. And they had the genius of Paul Shaffer and the crème de la crème of studio guys from Stax.

DAN AYKROYD: We would have no Blues Brothers if it weren't for Tom Malone and Paul Shaffer. They were the *Saturday Night Live* band members who basically suggested the hiring of Steve Cropper, Donald "Duck" Dunn, Matt "Guitar" Murphy, and Tom "Bones" Malone, the definitive artists from Stax. When they joined, they saw we were treating the music with reverence and respect. They gave their approval, and once we had them, we had a worthy section that was taken seriously in the music world. On that basis, John and I could be free to do the classic antics in the tradition of front men like Wynonie Harris and Cab Calloway.

Paul Shaffer may be better known as David Letterman's sidekick and musical director, but he was also great on SNL, and every fan of the Blues Brothers knows he was their bandleader for two hit albums and a successful tour.

PAUL SHAFFER: Dan and John did it with the same sense of humor that they brought to *SNL* and eventually their blockbuster movie. They featured the greats of rhythm and blues, their idols, and in so many cases gave them a second life. Take Aretha Franklin, for example—she wasn't in fashion like she had been in 1967, but they revived her career. James Brown was also very vocal about what they did for him. Many artists understood that the Blues Brothers had a take on their music that was respectful, and that it was an opportunity for John and Dan to give back, to say, "This is what you did for us, and we're thankful for it."

The Godfather of Soul, James Brown, was one of those appreciative artists, and when he met Jim Belushi, aka Zee Blues, he expressed his gratitude for Jim's older brother, and original Blues Brother, John Belushi.

JIM BELUSHI: He said, "You know, your brother is a very special man. I was down. Nobody would work with me. Nobody would hire me, and your brother put me in *The Blues Brothers* movie. He would come to my trailer and help me with my lines. Your brother is a shining star up there right now, looking down upon you, and you have it too. And God bless your brother, and God bless you." I mean, he brought me to tears talking

HOUSE OF BLUES

1204 CAROLINE ST. • HOUSTON TX

888-40-BLUES • WWW.HOUSEOFBLUES.COM

JUNE 21

Buy tickets at LiveNation.com, HouseOfBlues.com, the box office, or call 877-598-6671

poster ©charliehardwick.com

about my brother. And that's why I realized he *is* the Godfather of Soul, not just music but of the soul.

BOBBY RUSH: When I saw the Blues Brothers, I felt the same way I did when I first saw Elvis Presley. You see, a lot of people kind of had lockjaw when they saw Elvis Presley because they thought he was imitating a black guy. If you knew Elvis Presley on a personal basis, he wasn't imitating anybody. It was just his personality. Maybe they put on the suits because that's what John Lee Hooker did, but they did it because they liked the music, man! I don't know where I or people like me would have been without them. These guys kept the blues going. I thank God for Dan Aykroyd, and I've heard all the sweet and respectful things he says about me, things I'll never forget as long as I live.

Tragedy came in 1982 when John Belushi was discovered dead of an apparent drug overdose in Bungalow 3 at the Chateau Marmont. Isaac Tigrett was in England when Dan Aykroyd came looking for a respite from the press.

ISAAC TIGRETT: As far as Dan was concerned, the Blues Brothers was over when John died. It took him a long time to get over it. It was a two-man show, and his partner, from one of the greatest partnerships show business has ever known, was gone. When I was looking to start House of Blues, I knew I needed a front man, and Dan Aykroyd as Elwood Blues was a natural to be the spokesman of House of Blues.

DAN AYKROYD: Isaac had the concept to do this chain of deluxe juke joints, and he married it with the Blues Brothers graphic, the one of John and me. It was the one drawing that was part of our branding and our symbology. He said, "There's life left in the Blues Brothers brand, so let's built a chain of clubs upon the legend of Jake and Elwood and their devotion to African American culture, music, art." And by combining something that the people already knew, that they could connect to and relate to, with a message of blues and antiestablishment,

he was able to appeal to members of the investment community.

ISAAC TIGRETT: The Blues Brothers is still a phenomenon. Go to Czechoslovakia and you'll see people dressed up as them. That's why they endure, because anyone can be a Blues Brother. All you have to do is put on a black suit, a fedora, and some sunglasses, and you've gone from an everyman to a Blues Brother. It's been so long since that movie, but everybody still loves it, and Dan became a national treasure because of it, so why not incorporate it into what we wanted to achieve with House of Blues?

DAN AYKROYD: It gave our people, our customers, the people walking in the door, an instant understanding of what the place is: It's a juke joint, and the Blues Brothers sanctioned it. And if you have the Blues Brothers, then you have blues artists, and blues artists lead to the root of rock and roll, and rock and roll leads to all music, and that's what House of Blues is—a house of all music. The Blues Brothers image is instant shorthand to all of that.

WARREN DeMARTINI of Ratt: The Blues Brothers movie was such a great thing. I was such a huge fan of the movie and Saturday Night Live, so when I heard they were building a club with that spirit I was really excited. And it was going to be a place that was really designed to sound good and be a great place to see a group—you don't really get that at many places. I remember the first time we played House of Blues. It had the same quality of picking up a vintage guitar—it just sounded right.

HOUSE OF BLUES GOES TO COLLEGE:
CAMBRIDGE HOUSE

DAN AYKROYD: *House of Blues* came out of the old John Lee Hooker album *House of the Blues*, and so did the look of the Blues Brothers: the fedora and the sunglasses.

ISAAC TIGRETT: That was somewhat of a coincidence that I found out later. The John Lee Hooker album was titled *House of the Blues*. When I named House of Blues, I was thinking of various fashion houses that referred to themselves as a "house," like "House of Dior" and others. It was confirmed in my mind when I saw a building in London off Trafalgar Square called "Canada House."

PAUL SHAFFER: When Danny first told me that he and Isaac were going to open their first one in Cambridge, Massachusetts, he said, "It's going be a place where we do live music every night." I said, "How can I be a part of it?" What more does one want in a nightclub, especially in an era when it was all electronic dance music. This was the early '90s, when it was all about the clubs and the DJ as the mixmaster playing prerecorded music, so I loved the dedication to the live music aspect.

Not everyone was as confident in the concept as Dan Aykroyd and Paul Shaffer. As Shaffer says, in a world of ravers and grunge rock scenes, why would anyone want to invest in a blues club?

MICHAEL GROZIER: Eventually that would become a big deal for House of Blues—keeping contemporary while honoring the blues. Paul's right—techno music was starting to come out, and kids were getting into grunge, so how do you do that while paying tribute to a lifestyle and the legacy of blues?

ISAAC TIGRETT: I saw a need for live music and knew it was going to make a comeback. And together with bringing back live music, we were going to raise the consciousness about African American culture. The name *House of Blues* was intended to be a statement that said jazz, rock and roll, hard rock, rap, and everything else comes out of the blues. I'll tell you something: Except for Danny and later Paul, nobody would go along with me, despite how successful I was with the Hard Rock. Here I am, "Mr. Hard Rock," with one of the biggest brands in the world, and no one would believe in me. "Oh, we get the rock and roll," they'd tell me, "but blues music? Blues only sells forty thousand records a year in the United States. It's dead, a bunch of old-time shit from the '40s and '50s." I went from banker to banker, and no one got it. I knew this opportunity was with the blues, but how do we do this and where do we begin?

Little by little Isaac Tigrett found kindred spirits, if not in India with Sai Baba (where he would meet future HOB sculptor Andrew Wood, as well as his personal "chief of staff," Mark Princi), then in a restaurant in Sweden, where he became enamored with its manager, Nigel Shanley, and his sense of hospitality.

ANDREW WOOD: I remember Danny and Isaac were originally going to call it the B.B. Blues Bar.

NIGEL SHANLEY: If I remember correctly, the dream was to call it the B.B. Blues Bar, named after the bar Dan Aykroyd and John Belushi had, and I got word that Isaac bought this wonderful

TOP LEFT: Elwood Blues showing off HOB Cambridge.

blue house in Cambridge. An old lady owned it, and, as Isaac is apt to do, he overpaid by a fortune. And then I believe phone calls were made by B.B. King's people, and their attitude was you can't do something like B.B. Blues Bar, it's too close to B.B. King's Blues Club. Obviously Isaac had high regard for B.B. King and all the blues guys, and without any qualms Isaac said, "We're not calling it B.B. Blues Bar; we're calling it House of Blues." Dan Aykroyd's idea was a little bar; Isaac's dream and talent made it a world-renowned name.

MARK PRINCI: Isaac was a global figure and an amazing success story, so he had a fine track record, and Danny had the entertainment and music world in his pocket—together they went looking for venture capitalists. And the investors said, "Well, we don't really get it; show us what you mean."

ISAAC TIGRETT: It took me about five minutes to realize that if I opened it in Harvard Square in Cambridge, we could tap into a truly international market. The reason I wanted Cambridge was because there's 700,000 students in the Boston area and Harvard Square was ground zero. Sixty percent of them are the brightest and the best from all over the world—you walk across Harvard Square and you hear four languages spoken. I said, "If we're going to break a brand internationally, I want them to get used to this brand at ground zero." That's 150,000 new freshmen every year, and I said, "They'll take this and spread the word all over the world." I never spent a dime on advertising for House of Blues,

ABOVE: B.B. King at HOB Atlantic City, September 2005.

ever, not five cents, because that's like calling for help if you're in the culture business.

Harvard University more than welcomed Isaac Tigrett into the neighborhood. The university broke off a chunk of its $6 billion endowment via the Aeneas Group and became his second-largest investor, next to old family friend Sir James Goldsmith (or "Uncle Jimmy" to Tigrett). River Phoenix, John Candy, Judy Belushi, Dan Aykroyd, and Tigrett himself bankrolled the rest.

ISAAC TIGRETT: I also had to get Don Law's permission before I could move into Boston. He was the most powerful promoter in Boston, and his father recorded Robert Johnson for RCA! I came to him and said, "We're primarily doing blues music and we're not going to be a threat to you, and you're not going to control it." This was the first time he ever let anyone through the cracks, and I'm very grateful to him.

It was time to build House of Blues. Not only to give birth to a brand but to physically construct—if not from the ground up, at least from the inside out—a new house. It started small, not with a warehouse or a theater but with a house at 96 Winthrop Street, known as the Cambridge House. All Isaac Tigrett had to do was get it ready for opening, which required coming up with logos and reconstruction and curating the space. The logos wouldn't be a problem, not when Tigrett had his guru, Sai Baba, and Beatles graphic designer Alan Aldridge.

ISAAC TIGRETT: It was Sai Baba who chose the Sacré-Coeur [Sacred Heart] for the original House of Blues logo. I was freaking out and said, "Swami, this is a sacred symbol!" But he said it would be fine because it represents the pain and suffering that African Americans had to go through. So I said, "Fine; I'm making it the logo for House of Blues."

TOP: The artful greenroom at HOB Cambridge was a treat for touring musicians.
OPPOSITE: The Bluesmobile in front of HOB Cambridge on opening night.

Sai Baba also brought in Andrew Wood. Wood is responsible for the iconic sculpture reliefs—portraits of the greats in blues and rock and roll—you see on the walls and ceilings of House of Blues. Isaac Tigrett was already familiar with his work and had collaborated with both Wood and Mark Princi in the design and build of the Sri Sathya Sai Institute of Higher Medical Sciences—a hospital that was built (in one year, just as they promised their guru) to provide much-needed health care to the impoverished people of South India.

ANDREW WOOD: I remember Danny and Isaac were originally going to call it the B.B. Blues Bar. I was asked to make a ceiling of reliefs commemorating the blues gods, and I made one of Albert King as a prototype. I devised a format where each one would be twenty-eight inches square. It was challenging at the time because you couldn't just Google Bobby "Blue" Bland. I had to go off photos, and most of those had a lot of shadows, which made it even harder to invent the space. Because, you see, relief sculpture is all about trying to conjure that third dimension. We made about fifty or sixty of them for Cambridge. What was also interesting to me was that the first LP I ever bought as a boy in England was John Lee Hooker's *House of the Blues*.

House of Blues Cambridge opened its doors to the public on November 26, 1992, but opening festivities started several days before and went on for several days after. Among other comfort foods, the menu featured tandoori chicken, jambalaya, quesadillas, pizza, and local favorites such as catfish nuggets and blue clam chowder. On opening night Elwood Blues came screeching up in his Bluesmobile and delivered a speech that started the evening on a respectful note, reminding everyone that his mission as a servant to the blues had never changed. "We feel very honored to be here in this academic community," he began. "You'll see our club is a celebration of African American vitality." He then went on to explain how the blues had never left, how it appeared to him when he first heard Led Zeppelin, and how it's there every time a kid picks up a guitar. Steve Cropper also gave Isaac Tigrett and House of Blues some love when he said, "I think it's a great idea what Isaac Tigrett is intending to do in terms of educating the public and the new generation in the blues, and to give them a place to experience the blues."

BOBBY RUSH: The blues is a state of mind. When I was growing up, on Friday afternoon we knew Saturday was coming the next day and we were happy. Although we were going to the juke joint, to the little hole in the wall, we were happy about it.

MICHAEL GROZIER: Of course, Dan Aykroyd had the Blues Brothers band backing him. Then we had Joe Walsh; Luther "Guitar Junior" Johnson, who was amazing; Eddie Floyd; and Paul Rodgers from Bad Company. And I remember Andrew Strong, who was the singer in the Commitments.

PAUL SHAFFER: All the openings were magnificent evenings, but we did this ceremony where all of us musicians put our hands and asses into wet concrete. That remained outside the club throughout its existence. The Cambridge House was a small club, maybe experimental, to see how it would work.

ISAAC TIGRETT: Dan and I got all the musicians, about thirty of them—the Stax guys, Aerosmith, cats from Chicago—to get into long johns and do "butt prints" like they do at Grauman's Chinese Theatre. But I'll tell you, one of the highlights was Andrew Strong from the Commitments—what an incredibly soulful voice. He did "Mustang Sally" that night—the kid was so fucking good! We created a 1950s-style poster for everyone who played there, and the opening night ended up going for a solid eight hours. It was unbelievable! We didn't plan it right because nobody wanted to get off the stage—it just went on and on.

DAN AYKROYD: I remember thinking, "Boy, this place is small. How are we going to manage the crowds waiting outside? How is everyone going to be satisfied and happy?" I was worried about the capacity that night, because it was such a popular opening and everybody in the entire city could feel the buzz of what was going on and what was coming to town. It was a completely new, real venue for blues music devoted to local artists, regional artists, and national artists with the best blues booker in the business, Teo Leyasmeyer. Somehow everybody crammed in there, and it was packed to the rafters, even up the stairs to the washroom doors, because there was no place else to stand. The balcony overlooking the back of the house toward the stage was absolutely packed, the bars were packed, the downstairs was packed, and it was such an exciting night because the music delivered and the people felt like they were part of an electric scene.

TOP LEFT: Little Sammy Davis on the harp at HOB Cambridge. BOTTOM RIGHT: Grammy Award–winning bluesman Sugar Blue on the harmonica at HOB Cambridge. His harp can be heard on numerous blues and rock albums, most famously on the Rolling Stones tune "Miss You."

Among those who kept the party going was fourteen-year-old guitar wizard "Little Mikey." The kid was such an animal on the ax that Dan Aykroyd dubbed him "Monster" Mike Welch—a big handle for a teen, and one that's stuck ever since.

NIGEL SHANLEY: His mother had to come in with him to gigs because it was illegal to have a minor in a club without supervision. I remember Isaac took him in and created a record label just for him—he became our guy, and part of the house band.

"THE PLACE WAS ALWAYS COMPLETELY PACKED, AND IT WAS ALWAYS FILLED WITH ENERGY."
—*SHEMEKIA COPELAND*

SHEMEKIA COPELAND: It was the absolute best. The place was always completely packed. You know, New England people are the best blues fans ever, and it was always just totally filled with energy. I don't know why, but it's always been one of the best markets for the blues and was one of my dad's best markets for many years. It's a good spot for music. My father loved House of Blues Cambridge, and we were always excited to go up there. It was very welcoming and warm, and the size of it was perfect for blues artists. That House of Blues was perfect.

Like "Monster" Mike, Blues diva Shemekia Copeland—daughter of dearly departed blues hero Johnny "Clyde" Copeland—grew up in House of Blues Cambridge. She came of age watching her father play there, joined him onstage there, and eventually commanded many a House of Blues stage on her own. But that's not unusual. House of Blues took root in Cambridge and would soon branch out to other cities across the nation, where its stages not only would host the most important names in music but also would inevitably become breeding grounds for a generation of influential and adored artists to come.

LEFT: (Left to right) Jim Belushi, Dan Aykroyd, and John Goodman as Zee Blues, Elwood Blues, and Mighty Mack McTeer.
TOP RIGHT: Chicago blues guitarist and singer Hubert Sumlin performing at HOB Cambridge.

chapter two

BAD BOYS FROM BOSTON:
HOUSE OF BLUES GETS ITS WINGS

ROM THE MOMENT they opened the doors, House of Blues Cambridge took off like a jet from a Logan Airport runway. Isaac Tigrett and Dan Aykroyd's B.B. Blues Bar offered local students the antidote to the techno-raving megaclubs and "alternative" hole-in-the-wall dives of the time. The student body showed up in droves to the 220-seat juke joint, and the three seatings at its Sunday Gospel Brunch were selling out by noon the previous Monday. "I never thought I'd see a bunch of Yankees all holding hands, singing hallelujah, and carrying on with tears in their eyes," Tigrett later told *Forbes* magazine's Dana Wechsler Linden. With the successful launch of the Cambridge House, Tigrett was able to attract more investors, such as the Bad Boys from Boston themselves, Aerosmith (who showed up opening night, presumably to get their feet wet), along with singer Carly Simon and George Wendt, better known as "Norm" from *Cheers*.

NIGEL SHANLEY: Aerosmith showed up quickly because of Isaac's rock-and-roll connections, but since Isaac had so many things to do, I was the one who schmoozed them. One night they came down when we had two big blues guys onstage—I think they were Albert Collins and Robert Cray. Of course, Aerosmith were huge stars, so I needed to rope off a section for them. Then they got up to leave after the first act, which slightly disappointed me, but on the way out Steven Tyler said, "Nigel, who can beat what we just saw? I mean, that was out of this world!" They were so cool, and they soon became involved in a small way financially.

ISAAC TIGRETT: Aerosmith couldn't move fast enough to be a part of the team, and they were so immersed in House of Blues that they wanted to do a blues album. Joe Perry talked about all the blues guys they were influenced by, and they were in awe of Dan Aykroyd . . . everybody was.

DAN AYKROYD: I think Aerosmith are still happy with their association with House of Blues. But the thing about Boston that made it a really huge success was our booker, Teo. He was one of the greatest impresarios. He knew all the people in the blues and R&B world, toured as a pianist with Buddy Guy, and gave us so much in terms of building the value of the company. He's deceased now, but he was a great man.

OPPOSITE: Though known as a pioneer of the electric Chicago blues sound, here Buddy Guy is putting on an acoustic performance at HOB L.A.

DAVE FORTIN: I would get frustrated and at the same time enthralled listening to Teo on the phone in the bustling office. He'd spend an hour talking to one manager or one artist because that connection was real—it was more than just business, it was about the culture and the passion he had for blues. He knew about their families, their lives, and when he was talking to them he was an active part of it. It wasn't business to him, it was just who he was. No one went above and beyond for the artists more than Teo. He'd head to the airport himself to pick up guys like Johnny "Clyde" Copeland, Guy Davis, Taj Mahal, Solomon Burke, Dr. John, Luther Allison, Jimmy Smith, and Lou Rawls, to name just a few, because he wanted to set the right tone and show respect. To Teo, it was all about family, this family of musicians performing from a place so deep in their soul, so authentic, that you couldn't imagine them not onstage pouring their hearts out.

ISAAC TIGRETT: Teo was a beloved blues master and a terrific piano player who had played with the greats, including Muddy Waters. He knew them all, and they trusted his involvement as a fellow player. He was truly respected by everyone, a fine soul, and so much more knowledgeable than any of us at the start. He made Cambridge happen.

All week long, students from Harvard and other nearby universities could get down with Otis Rush, Solomon Burke, Dr. John, Ike Turner, and the Blind Boys of Alabama. And this was due in no small part to the venue's resident blues expert and talent buyer, Teo Leyasmeyer. Leyasmeyer not only had established relationships with musicians, but he also helped determine how House of Blues would engage with the musicians who worked their stages. By many accounts, including those of Dave Fortin, who started as a bar back and is now VP of marketing for Live Nation, Leyasmeyer treated his fellow musicians with love and respect, often telling them to go home after a gig to rest and come back the next day, when his stage crew would assist them with a load-out and often treat them to another meal. House of Blues would soon become known for its artist-friendly environment; it was often the tour stop that bands would most look forward to.

TOP LEFT: Steven Tyler of Aerosmith during Aerosmith Live at House of Blues in L.A., 1994. BOTTOM RIGHT: Teo Leyasmeyer (left) and Johnny "Clyde" Copeland, HOB Cambridge. OPPOSITE: Chicago blues–style harmonica player Carey Bell performing at HOB Cambridge. In addition to his own albums, Bell recorded with other blues legends such as Robert Nighthawk and Louisiana Red.

SHEMEKIA COPELAND: Teo played in my father's [Johnny "Clyde" Copeland's] band for many years, and after my dad passed he would bring me up there to do gigs. Teo definitely knew what the music was all about. Any place that would have a guy like Teo running it totally gets it.

Kevin Morrow, winner of three consecutive Pollstar Nightclub Talent Buyer of the Year awards as the head talent buyer for House of Blues (eventually becoming House of Blues senior vice president and later president of Live Nation, New York, before forming his own Steel Wool Entertainment), also knew how valuable Teo Leyasmeyer was in those early days.

KEVIN MORROW: Teo was a bluesologist who probably knew more about blues than any other booker in our system. And not only blues; he knew all the gospel and soul musicians as well. He could have easily written a book about the

blues because he really knew his history. Plus, he was a super nice human being.

DAVE FORTIN: The quality of acts that Teo got to perform at the original House of Blues was just incredible. And he got *everyone* through the club that he could from the blues side. The journeymen of the blues business were the most dear to him—the acts on the road—some of them playing two hundred nights a year. Guitar Shorty, Lonnie Smith, Pinetop Perkins, Little Milton—the list could go on forever. For some of the guys, after a gig Teo would reach into his own pocket and give them a little extra something—like you would do for a family member. Without a thought, he'd just send them on their way knowing they'd get a good meal in before the next gig.

STRETCHIN' OUT:

HARVARD SQUARE TO THE SUNSET STRIP

With a happening juke joint, the brand was able to grow almost immediately: There were House of Blues Radio Hour *(a collaboration with CBS); a record label, House of Blues Records (a collaboration with BMG); and a TV show in development (*Live from House of Blues *would soon be a weekly show on TBS). With more investors in tow, it was time to secure additional locations for House of Blues.*

MICHAEL GROZIER: From that little 220-capacity club, we raised $35 million in venture capital to open New Orleans and Los Angeles, and we were working on buying a property in New York. The original plan was to open three or four locations. We opened Boston, we had a lease on New Orleans, then we had a lease for the Sunset Strip, and we also had a piece of property under option in Chicago.

ISAAC TIGRETT: I wanted House of Blues to raise the consciousness about African American culture and about the fact that out of blues came jazz, rock and roll, hard rock, hip-hop, and everything else. When I hired Kevin Morrow I said, "This is what we're going to do: We're going to fill these places up with all styles of music every night of the week! And we will keep R&B, jazz, and the Gospel Brunch because we started that in Cambridge."

ABOVE: Rod Piazza, HOB Cambridge. Piazza and his group the Mighty Flyers are known for their boogie and West Coast blues sound.

NEW ORLEANS (January 1994)

"There is a house in New Orleans . . ." goes the maudlin standard, but Eric Burdon and the Animals might have been singing a different tune if they'd skipped the House of the Rising Sun and partied at House of Blues instead, which opened in NOLA in January 1994 in the heart of the world-famous French Quarter. Its status on Decatur Street proved that one didn't have to stick to the familiar Bourbon Street to find a great party.

The festive, swamp-bound, mysterious, and colorful city emitted just the right vibe for a juke joint looking to expand and evolve without losing its roots in blues or its unique aesthetic. As author Tom Robbins describes, "New Orleans listens eagerly to the seductive promises of the future but keeps at least one foot firmly planted in its history, and in the end, conforms, like an artist, not to the world but to its own inner being—ever mindful of its personal style," which could just as easily be said of House of Blues as it began to spread its wings. Looking to the future, but not forgetting the origins of its inspiration, House of Blues set its sights on becoming much more than just a blues venue—and had to if it was to fill its larger physical footprint and expand its influence. Head talent buyer of House of Blues New Orleans, Sonny Schneidau, remembers the transition well as he recalls not only why his hometown was the perfect place for a second venue but also why there was a need to make some early adjustments in booking styles.

SONNY SCHNEIDAU: New Orleans is one of the great musical cities, if not the greatest musical city, in America. There are so many traditions in New Orleans: jazz, spiritual music, Mardi Gras, Indian music, and our neighbors to the west have zydeco and Cajun music. Louisiana has always been very fertile musical ground. Cambridge was such a small club and really true to the blues, and Teo Leyasmeyer—one of my dear friends and one of the kindest gentlemen I have ever known—really guided that venue; I would say that 95 percent of its programming was local and touring midlevel blues stuff, with the exception of the bigger nights when Isaac and Dan would bring in some headliners. But it's different opening a one-thousand-seat club in New Orleans, and it was a little bit of a challenge to decide what kind of music we were going to program and what music would work, because

we knew the club wouldn't survive on the blues alone. There was a bit of a learning curve about how to deal with the kinds of shows that were going to come in on a regular basis, but Isaac used to always quote Willie Dixon's famous line, "The blues are the roots and the rest are the fruits."

Along with a more eclectic musical palette, a couple of new traditions began at the New Orleans House of Blues: first was the "Mississippi Mud Pour" (the ceremony of burying a few shovelsful of dirt from the Crossroads of the Mississippi Delta in a metal box underneath the stage and at the entrance of each venue), and the second was having James Brown headline one of the opening nights.

DAN AYKROYD: Every time James opened up House of Blues, we would have a private moment together after the show in his dressing room. I would always present him with a maple leaf and a one-ounce gold sovereign coin. He opened six of the clubs, so there are at least six of those coins. That was my way of respecting him.

ABOVE LEFT: The famous Blues Brothers Bluesmobile. **TOP RIGHT:** Facade of HOB New Orleans with local hero and blues legend Clarence "Gatemouth" Brown overseeing the entrance.

SONNY SCHNEIDAU: James Brown headlined one night, but I remember more clearly the night Gatemouth headlined. We also booked legends like Robert Cray, Buddy Guy, Tito Puente, Solomon Burke, Bobby "Blue" Bland, Jackson Browne, Koko Taylor, and Sheila E. And that was just the first year in New Orleans!

MICHAEL GROZIER: Local hero and blues legend Clarence "Gatemouth" Brown was like our patron saint in New Orleans. He was a guitar player, a fiddle player, and an old crotchety motherfucker—and proud to be one, too. There was nobody like him. When Eric Clapton played New Orleans he made sure to bring Gatemouth onstage with him. We even gave him his own booth, which we commemorated with a crest-shaped plaque that hangs over the table. One day he came in, and he was, like, "Man, why don't you take some of that shit down and put some of my artwork up?" I said, "Sure, Gate, whatever you want." So he came back with these steer antlers, which we put up over his booth,

as well as a portrait somebody did of him riding a horse on the edge of a cliff, striking down the devil, like it was him against Satan and he was winning! Gatemouth would also smoke this corn pipe with a mixture of tobacco and pot, and I remember him loving our catfish bites, which he would eat with honey while sitting in his booth and sipping tea.

John Goodman lived in New Orleans, and one day he came by to hang out and we sat in Gate's booth. Somebody that worked for us said, "You know, if Gatemouth was here he'd throw you out of his booth." John Goodman laughed. Sure enough, twenty minutes later, Gatemouth shows up and says, "Boy! You better get out of my booth! Don't make me take out my pistol!"

SONNY SCHNEIDAU: I saw that story happen with Goodman and dozens of other people throughout the years—if somebody was sitting in Gate's booth we would literally have to relocate them because he'd say, "Hey, you're

---

TOP: Gatemouth performing at HOB New Orleans. Failing health required he use an oxygen tank, but that didn't stop him from bringing down the house.

HOUSE OF BLUES RECORDS

Some say the decision to start up House of Blues Records was made the second a thirteen-year-old Mikey Welch walked into the Cambridge House of Blues, plugged in his guitar, and belted out his signature "Monster" sound. "Monster" Mike Welch would be the very first artist signed to House of Blues' brand-new label in August 1994. A joint venture with Private Music (an imprint of BMG Music Group) and the newly created House of Blues Music Company, it became a bona fide full-service music entity, discovering and A&Ring new talent, handling their publicity, and even recording their music at House of Blues Studios. While looking for and recording the blues stars of tomorrow (like "Monster" Mike Welch and Derek Trucks), House of Blues Records was also busy releasing studio albums by perennial artists such as Roger Daltrey, the Blind Boys of Alabama, and Otis Rush and live albums that represented the many different types of acts that have performed on a House of Blues stage, such as Blondie, the Blues Brothers, and Tupac. When added up, there are well over one hundred releases. But the most critically acclaimed and collectible of the House of Blues records are probably the tribute albums (like those to the Rolling Stones, Bob Dylan, and Janis Joplin) and the exhaustive compilations (such as the *Essential* series), with *Essential Blues 2* making *Billboard*'s list of Top Blues Albums in 1996. After becoming a dedicated collector of the catalog himself, writer Tom Tourville noted in *The House of Blues Music Release Story: The Holy Grail of Blues Music Releases* in 2010, "I soon learned that any release on the House of Blues label was as close to a musical masterpiece as one could find."

50,000 WATTS OF HOUSE OF BLUES RADIO POWER

House of Blues Radio Hour (now called *The Blues Mobile with Elwood Blues* or simply *The Blues Mobile*) hit the airwaves in 1993, shortly after Dan Aykroyd took the stage with harmonica master Charlie Musselwhite—who was also a template for Aykroyd's Elwood Blues character—for the opening of the first House of Blues in Cambridge, Massachusetts. Elwood Blues tells the story on *The Blues Mobile*'s website: "Later, Charlie ran into his buddy, radio producer Ben Manilla, who said he was thinking of starting a syndicated blues radio show. Manilla passed the secret initiation ritual, and together we conned CBS Radio into letting us have airtime." It was a little more complicated than that—but not much, as it's mostly a tale of synchronicity. As Musselwhite's manager, Kevin Morrow, recalls, "In one afternoon, in about two hours, we put together the House of Blues Radio Casting Network, which began with Ben Manilla, Michael Murphy [who was hired to look for branding opportunities for the newly minted House of Blues Entertainment], and myself."

House of Blues Radio Hour may have changed its name, but it's Dan Aykroyd's continuing mission to educate listeners about the influence his favorite blues masters had on popular rock acts that continues to motivate both House of Blues and the radio show. And twenty years later, Ben Manilla is just as passionate about what they do. "The concept that I sold to CBS—and that Dan agreed to, and that we've pretty much adhered to—is that if you like the Rolling Stones, if you like the White Stripes, if you like Led Zeppelin, Aerosmith, or Eric Clapton, then guess what? You like the blues—because all these people play blues music."

Now the longest-running blues radio show in radio history, it's won the International Radio Festival's "Best of Show," The Grand Award—twice. "It is significant," explains Manilla, "because it truly is international. The festival includes NBC, BBC, CBC, NPR—all of the radio outlets. And we also won *Billboard* magazine's Syndicated Radio Show of the Year Award." The year 2004 saw another collaboration from Dan Aykroyd and Ben Manilla with their book, *Elwood's Blues: Interviews with the Blues Legends and Stars* (from Backbeat Books), which is composed entirely of interviews from the radio show. Looking back at the success of *House of Blues Radio Hour* and its continuation as *The Blues Mobile*, Manilla concludes, "Certainly the production played a big part of it. But it would be nowhere without Dan Aykroyd—without Elwood Blues—without him being the actor that he is and a passionate spokesman."

TOP: The 2006 WWOZ Piano Night at HOB New Orleans featured Eddie Bo, Marcia Ball, Joe Crown, Cindy Chen, and many more. The annual benefit falls between the two New Orleans Jazz & Heritage Festival weekends.

sitting in my booth!" We hung up horns on the wall right there so Gate could hang up his hat! He was a wonderful bandleader, a consummate professional, a master musician, and a multi-instrumentalist. He was a one-of-a-kind guy and was sort of our patron saint; in some ways he adopted us.

ISAAC TIGRETT: We had Gatemouth's booth done in all leopard. It was totally against everything we did, but he was a genius. Of course, you can't bring up New Orleans without talking about the Neville Brothers, who we had every Mardi Gras, and Dr. John—all so incredible. I love Dr. John. He was wonderful to us; he knew my wife, Maureen, back in the Beatles days when she was married to Ringo Starr. In fact, when he heard I was starting to do the memorabilia thing, he gave me his cane with a carved skull on the top of it.

DR. JOHN: A lot of my memories warp together like some kind of Salvador Dalí painting, but I have fond memories of sitting on the bus with Isaac and his wife, outside of House of Blues in New Orleans, just having a good time! You know, Isaac married Ringo's ex-wife, Maureen Starkey, and one time back in London I gave her one of my walking sticks.

MICHAEL GROZIER: L.A. was still in construction when we opened up New Orleans, and we thought, "Wow, we've finally become an entertainment company that's doing food, as opposed to a restaurant company that's doing entertainment." It started with the opening of Boston, but by the time we opened New Orleans, we had the momentum and we knew we were on to something.

LOS ANGELES (March 1994)

The juke joint on the corner of Sunset Boulevard and Olive Drive has naturally distressed clapboards and a rusted corrugated tin roof that shakes, rattles, and rolls every night of the week. This cotton gin of a juke joint looks nothing like the Mondrian Hotel across one street, or the Comedy Store and the infamous "Riot House" across the other. It's just not "Hollywood," neither vintage Hollywood nor hipster Hollywood, despite its proximity to the equally storied Chateau Marmont. This juke joint looks like nothing else the town has ever seen . . . it's as if it crash-landed on the Sunset Strip by way of the levee-breaking force of a crossfire hurricane. The place emits an unmistakable mojo, and that's because, for the third installment of House of Blues, Isaac Tigrett took Highway 61 all the way back to the source, back to the Crossroads. There he gathered material from the old Stovall Plantation cotton gin, brought it to Tinseltown, and dropped an authentic juke joint in the heart of a not-so-glitzy Sunset Strip.

TOP: The facade of HOB L.A. is composed almost entirely of repurposed corrugated tin siding brought from the Crossroads.

ISAAC TIGRETT: The Sunset Strip was boarded up and filled with crack dealers when we moved into that location. The only places that were left were the old Whisky A Go-Go, the Roxy, the Rainbow, and the Troubadour over on Doheny Drive and Santa Monica Boulevard. But otherwise it was just a filth hole. The second we opened up, other clubs and restaurants followed. But before that, the Sunset Strip was literally worse than Hollywood Boulevard. The property itself was the old John Barrymore house, which had been derelict for years.

DAN AYKROYD: There were very few institutional buildings, except for the Mondrian, which was built in 1928, and the Chateau Marmont, built in 1926. Aside from a few apartment buildings the area was mainly private residences. The location is one that's always had a precedent of outrageous partying: When it was Roy's in the '70s, and you wanted to do some coke after your meal, they would put a bunch of coke on your credit card and charge you for a $50 "dessert." Its final reincarnation was as the annex of the Comedy Store, and a restaurant called Butterfield's.

BELOW, LEFT TO RIGHT: Though raised in rural Mississippi, Muddy Waters is considered the father of Chicago blues, bringing the Delta sound to urban communities and taking the musical form electric. Cotton gin/compress in Clarksdale where Tigrett found the corrugated siding for his Hollywood juke joint. Muddy Waters's cabin prior to the restoration undertaken by House of Blues.

DAN AYKROYD: When we tore [the original structure] down there were rats inside the walls and dry rot. We basically tore it to the ground and rebuilt it to earthquake specifications. There are pictures of the spot through the dead periods in the '80s, when a lot of the buildings were boarded up. Now it's a pedestrian destination—House of Blues started the revitalization of that part of L.A.

MELISSA ETHERIDGE: When they started building House of Blues on Sunset it was like, "What is that?" And then when they put up the tin roof it was like, "What the heck is this?" And then going in, the first thing that hit me, what really struck me, was all the art.

ISAAC TIGRETT: In the summer of 1993 I went to visit Danny when he was filming *Canadian Bacon* with John Candy. I saw the set builders make this old funky house, just like the juke joint I was making for the Sunset Strip, and I said, "This town is all about reasonable facsimiles. There's nothing authentic about this whole culture. I can't build a new 'old house' and get away with it." I prayed to my guru Sai Baba for help, just like I did when I opened every location. That night I had a dream about when I had gone down to the famous Crossroads in Clarksdale, Mississippi, where Robert Johnson supposedly sold his soul to the devil. There's a family down there, the Stovalls,

who were friends with my family, and they had one of the first cotton gins and cotton houses that were built in the '20s, when they discovered corrugated tin. The Stovall Plantation is the same estate where Muddy Waters had recorded for Alan Lomax and the Congressional Library—and it hit me: That's where I needed to go to make my juke joint on the Sunset Strip authentic.

Howard Stovall, executive director of the Blues Foundation, and a member the family who owned the plantation where Muddy Waters was discovered, remembers the transaction well.

HOWARD STOVALL: When Isaac came to Clarksdale collecting material for the Sunset Strip, he saw an enormous red tin-covered cotton gin/compress that was just a vacant building. He was like, "Whoa! I hit the mother lode!" Believe me, they were delighted to sell it to him. There was a lot of red tin on that building, more than we could give him from the old houses that were on our property.

ISAAC TIGRETT: Then I went by Muddy Waters's cabin, and I heard that a hurricane had just blown off the porch and the roof. I said to the Stovalls, "I want to take all the tin off that warehouse that you have over on Highway 61 and I'll replace it with brand-new tin." They thought I was out of my mind, like, "What's wrong with this Tigrett boy?"

HOWARD STOVALL: Isaac had the vision and the resources to make it a reality. He came down here at a time when very few people were paying attention to this stuff. There were guys like me and Billy Gibbons—who used some of the Muddy Waters cabin to make his "Muddywood" guitar—and James Jaworowicz, also of the Blues Foundation, but the fact that Isaac did it when nobody was doing it prompted all kinds of chambers of commerce to start recognizing the huge cultural asset they had right in their backyard.

ISAAC TIGRETT: I found out that that particular tin warehouse is where they took the bales of hay and where Muddy Waters worked as a kid, so I took every piece of tin, numbered it, and reassembled it as closely as I could for House of Blues. I also bought the Muddy Waters cabin, which was an old slave house built in the 1800s and where they recorded him when he was nineteen. Since it was falling apart and I'd need other pieces to supplement it, I bought the cabin next to it as well. If I hadn't bought it, the whole thing would have blown over. Architectural historians put it

back together, and eventually we put it on display at the Chicago Blues Festival and at the Atlanta Olympics as well. I made a deal with the Stovalls to give it back in a certain number of years because Howard knew how important it was.

If bringing a cotton gin from the Crossroads of Clarksdale, Mississippi, wasn't ambitious enough, Isaac Tigrett set about making another striking attraction, only this one would be on the inside: the Jake and Elwood Movable Bars, better known as the "swinging bars." And they were to make their debut on September 20, 1994, along with a special return to the stage by John Fogerty.

DAN AYKROYD: For the first night, Isaac and I wrote a heartfelt and convincing letter to John Fogerty saying, "You have to be the one that opens this club because you'll be able to get people who haven't seen you for so long to come in. You'll be able to really hammer home our point that House of Blues is a celebration of American and African American culture and how artists like you have interpreted the blues." And he said yes. So that first night I basically set up a private invitation to everyone who ran

ABOVE: James Brown performing at HOB L.A. in 2005. The Hardest-Working Man in Show Business, James Brown not only opened several House of Blues venues but also continued to perform until late in his life. He was seventy-two years old at the time of this performance. **OPPOSITE:** Muddy Waters's cabin restored for display at the 1996 Olympics. **PAGES 46–47:** James Brown feelin' good at HOB L.A. November 16, 2005.

HOUSE OF BLUES TAKES THE GOLD

The Games of the XXVI Olympiad, better known as the 1996 Summer Olympics, was another expansion opportunity for House of Blues, even if it was more of a pop-up than a permanent House. Isaac Tigrett secured the great Baptist Tabernacle, which was designed by famed architect R. H. Hunt (whose credits also included the Grand Ole Opry in Nashville) in 1907 and which opened in 1909. It didn't look like a juke joint, but there's no doubt it became a rock-and-roll church. The opening festivities began with the Blues Brothers (now with Jim Belushi and John Goodman) on July 19 and 20. The two-month lineup of artists showcased an immensity of talent, including the likes of James Brown, Johnny Cash, Al Green, Jerry Lee Lewis, Burning Spear, Third World, Tito Puente, Celia Cruz, and even one of Tigrett's all-time heroes, Bob Dylan.

"It was a little outpost of House of Blues that was only open during the Olympics," says Paul Shaffer, "and I remember it having a wonderful opening." Blues Brother Jim Belushi also has fond memories of the Summer Games. "Oh, yeah, that was magic, man! With James Brown and that big beautiful tabernacle, singing with the original Blues Brothers band. I met my girlfriend, now my wife, Jenny, that night. We pulled her up onstage and danced, and I've got a photo of it on my wall. And then Goodman, man! We came off the stage for a little break

and we had to give him an oxygen mask. I was like, 'You're turning gray, man!' But he would just go out there and give one hundred percent."

There were the Games, and then there were the fun and games that took place around the temporary venue's makeshift abode, located in the heart of Olympic Village. For starters, Isaac Tigrett arranged for the Muddy Waters cabin (yes, the one from the Crossroads that Alan Lomax came to visit when looking for Robert Johnson) to be on display; this was done to remind guests of America's musical heritage. Next, Tigrett welcomed the international press for one of the first cyber chats in an early cyber café: House of Blues–sponsored The Java Joint. While sipping on a cup of mud, journalists from all around the world could interview the many artists who would appear on a House of Blues stage, and they would in turn spread the word about the emerging entertainment company behind it. And last, but certainly not least, Mr. Foundation Room himself, Nigel Shanley (see chapter five for more on this legend), was put in charge of schmoozing in the not one but three temporary Foundation Rooms set up to entertain dignitaries and celebrities.

"That was my baby," Shanley explains with delight, telling how the Foundation Room in Atlanta was just as hot as the celebrity-filled private club in Los Angeles. "I was entertaining Michael Jordan, all the politicians—it became my show. I remember people trying to bribe me to get in—people from all around world, including leaders of small countries! Everybody came to House of Blues that summer: You either went to the Olympics or you came to us."

Hollywood—all the heads of studios, movie stars, writers, producers, directors in film and television—everybody. I sent them a note saying, "This night is for us. There will be no media, no press." There aren't any photos from that night because I banned cameras from the venue. I probably sent out about seven hundred invites, and they all came.

MICHAEL GROZIER: There were people eating dinner on the main floor and people up by the bar on the second floor. The bars were on these metal tracks, and the idea was that when the music started they would split open and one side of the bar would reposition on stage right and the other side would be moved to stage left, thus the "Jake and Elwood Bars." I don't think anyone had ever tried anything like that before; I mean it was an amazing work in progress.

It was Danny's party, and everybody in Hollywood was there—the A-list of the A-list.

There were three generations of the *SNL* cast there, from Chris Farley and David Spade to Billy Crystal and everyone from Dan's era. Clint Eastwood was there, along with Woody Harrelson, Wesley Snipes, Jack Nicholson—you get it? Let me rephrase, it was the 1 percent of the 1 percent. It was the first time that John Fogerty would play these songs in twenty years, and Isaac wanted to wait to open the bars until Disney's Michael Eisner and Michael Ovitz were there.

ISAAC TIGRETT: The idea of the swinging bars was to be able to combine the restaurant/bar with the nightclub. This way, instead of having people come only for dinner, they could stay for a show, and then they'd be in our environment for four hours instead of only one. So the idea was to have one bar that was about a hundred feet long. It was held up from the ceiling, and when the band would start these bars would split open in the middle and go into a little pocket on each side of the room, with the stage right below you. It blew people away.

DELTA CROSSROADS

THE METAL THAT ENSHRINES THIS HOUSE OF BLUES CAME FROM THE LEGENDARY "CROSSROADS" OF HIGHWAY 61 AND 49 OUTSIDE CLARKSDALE, MISSISSIPPI AT THESE CROSSROADS IN THE EARLY 1930'S DELTA BLUES MASTER ROBERT JOHNSON EVOKED SATAN AND SOLD HIS SOUL IN EXCHANGE FOR MUSICAL TALENT FAME AND FORTUNE HE THEN WROTE HIS INFAMOUS SONG CROSSROADS IMMORTALIZED OVER 30 YEARS LATER BY THE ENGLISH GROUP CREAM. HE DIED IN A MISSISSIPPI JUKE JOINT IN 1938 HIS GIN POISONED BY A JEALOUS LOVER

MICHAEL GROZIER: We were still working out the kinks all the way up to the opening. The bars were set to open when you pushed a button, but just in case, we'd have these huge guys waiting to pull on these gym ropes and manually open the bars if needed. Finally, Danny sent John Fogerty onto the stage and he started playing "Suzie Q."

KEVIN MORROW: Michael Ovitz and all these guys were up there, and the minute Dan said, "And welcome to the Eighth Wonder of the World—House of Blues!" I was on the walkie-talkie telling my guys to tell John Fogerty to "Hit it!" All of a sudden you heard this, "Do, do-do-do-do do, do-do-do-do" and . . .

MICHAEL GROZIER: Of course, we pushed the button and nothing happened. Another guy pushed the button and nothing. Then I got on the radio and yelled, "PULL! PULL! START PULLING THE ROPES!" So we opened it manually; it was amazing to watch it swing open.

KEVIN MORROW: When the bar started to open up, all of a sudden here we were floating over twelve hundred people, the curtains were opening at the exact same time, there was Fogerty for the first time in God knows how long, and he's playing "Susie Q"—it went off perfectly!

ISAAC TIGRETT: Nobody even knew it was John Fogerty because they hadn't seen him in years. Everybody was up on their feet and leaning over the bars, and Goldie Hawn was dancing on the table right below for the whole song.

PAUL SHAFFER: It was a huge night. Dan and I had a mutual friend who was getting married in Palm Springs that night, and so after sound check, Dan sent me on a private plane to Palm Springs so I could attend the wedding and then get back to the club. We went on at 11:00 p.m., and I think that was the first time they got that big mechanism [the swinging bars] to open up, right when it was time for the music to start. It was incredibly exciting.

BELOW: John Fogerty performing at HOB L.A. in February 2007.

CHICAGO (November 1996)

A rustic juke joint inside the body of an extravagant European-style opera house may be the best way to describe the masterpiece that is House of Blues Chicago. It's fitting that Isaac Tigrett chose the Marina City complex as the setting for the fourth and largest House of Blues venue at the time of its opening, on November 24, 1996. Straddling both sides of the Chicago River, the modern towers were erected in 1964 as a rejection of the "white flight" that was threatening metropolises everywhere. Financed by the Janitor's Union, a group of janitors and elevator operators proved you didn't have to be a Trump or come from a particular class to affect the skyline. It was an early case of the kind of urban redevelopment projects that have come to be expected from House of Blues, but the players doing the gentrification were just average Joes pulling together for something better. As with House of Blues' "Crazy Quilt," humble people stitched together and created a seamless community. A photo of Marina Towers appears on the sleeve art of Sly and the Family Stone's There's a Riot Goin' On, *and shortly before opening, House of Blues faced some rioters of its own when a flock of faithful Catholics showed up at the door in protest.*

ISAAC TIGRETT: As we approached the opening of Chicago, I was going nuts, worrying if I was about to lose my shirt. One day someone showed me a letter that came in from the Archdiocese of Chicago. I was too busy to look and dismissed it. A little time passed and then it was the morning after election day, November 6, 1996. The morning paper arrived, and I was expecting to see Bill Clinton and my childhood friend Al Gore on the front page, but instead the headline was something like "Cardinal Denies Evil Club . . ." The big story wasn't about the election but the fact that House of Blues was using the Sacré Coeur!

DAN AYKROYD: We really had trouble in Chicago with the Catholic Diocese when they saw that we were appropriating the Sacred Heart. But the Sacred Heart was a totally appropriate conveyance of our message and our branding because, really, if you look you'll find that the blues goes back to gospel, and gospel goes back to worshipping God. Gospel is an appeal to have God in our lives, and so the Sacred Heart was a totally appropriate way to show our House of Blues as being a spiritual house.

ISAAC TIGRETT: I finally opened the letter and read the official complaint. The fact that I had put it off for so long looked as if I were snubbing them. When I walked over to House of Blues at 7 a.m., there were around fifteen people protesting with signs, soon to be joined by another fifty, all yelling and giving me death threats. I'd already made friends with the mayor and I had my liquor license, permits from the fire department, the police department, the building department, everybody. But Chicago is a town of Catholics,

OPPOSITE: Facade of HOB Chicago. Built in a European-style opera house, the venue pays tribute to what Tigrett calls "America's original opera," the blues. ABOVE LEFT: HOB Chicago boasts two stories of luxury boxes. TOP RIGHT: Lead singer of The Used, Bert McCracken, performing at HOB Chicago.

all from Ireland, and as their beloved Cardinal was about to die, all they were hearing was that Isaac Tigrett and House of Blues was evil for exploiting the sacred symbol to make money. One by one the fire chief, the police chief—everybody—stepped up to me saying, "Sorry, but I'm going to have to take that permit back." I thought I was going have a heart attack and die on the spot.

NIGEL SHANLEY: I remember having to go to the Archdiocese with Isaac and thinking that they were expecting a bruising from a club owner, yet here's Isaac, who exudes love and peace, even though he's dressed all in black. We arrived and they started the attack, saying, "If you don't change the logo we will have demonstrations outside your building for weeks, for months, forever!" And, I tell you, I saw a glimmer in Isaac's eye almost wishing for that kind of free publicity, but he was calm and peaceful and agreed to alter the logo. I always made the joke that the logo went from the bleeding heart of Jesus to an inflamed liver, which is pretty appropriate when you think about it.

DAN AYKROYD: We removed some of the blood, and I think we removed the thorns [from the logo]. I think that assuaged the Catholic Church at the time. But eventually that logo evolved to the more stylized House of Blues logo that we see today, where there's the flame, the heart—it's not just a Christian symbol anymore. But I always thought the original logo was totally appropriate.

ISAAC TIGRETT: I know the Chicago Archdiocese was really intimidated by Dean James Morton coming all the way from New York and defending my character. And he did another thing for me that I'll never forget: He had the Cardinal write a letter saying that Isaac Tigrett is a good man and did not use the Sacred Heart sacrilegiously and has tremendous background helping the Church and others. I mean, we won, baby! I won't even talk about not believing in God after that, because we were in Chicago, the home of the Blues Brothers, and we really were on a mission from God! And all of a sudden in came Mayor Daley, the fire department, the police department—and all my permits!

"THE BLUES IS AMERICA'S ORIGINAL OPERA!"
—ISAAC TIGRETT

After it was all worked out, the parties issued dual press releases: one from Tigrett stating that "the chain's new heart symbol is described as an unfolding rose representing five basic human values: love, peace, truth, righteousness, and nonviolence," and the other from the Chicago Archdiocese, which said that it appreciated the restaurant's efforts to change the logo and "is satisfied that Mr. Tigrett and House of Blues did not mean to offend Catholics or people of faith by this use of the sacred symbol." The line that Isaac Tigrett appreciated the most? Probably the one at the end that hyped, "Chicago's House of Blues opens Nov. 24 at Marina Towers." With the controversy settled, the attention shifted to the sheer beauty of the operatic location.

ISAAC TIGRETT: For me, the two most important locations are New Orleans and Chicago—they are the two ends of the blues. I remember looking at the Chicago location and thinking about what we were going to do with it, and I closed my eyes and it came to me instantly: Chicago is where the blues went electric with the sounds of Muddy Waters and Buddy Guy, and then I was suddenly taken back to Europe, where my mother went to the famous Teatro alla Scala opera house in Milano. My mother was on the board of the Metropolitan Opera, and so from the age of thirteen I would go to New York and see the operas with her. I had seen Pavarotti and Domingo there, and I remember sitting there crying. And then it occurred to me that the blues is America's original opera! I mean, it's the same thing—all the stories are about tragedy and problems with relationships, like stealing wives and tales of jealousy, revenge, and murder. So we decided to build an opera house for the blues. We put in all these luxurious boxes, and before we even opened, all the boxes sold out—that's two stories of luxury boxes!

JIM BELUSHI: The Chicago House of Blues is the temple. I mean it is the juke joint opera house. Isaac got in a lot of trouble for that one because he spent a lot of money, but it is a monument, and I'm glad he spent the money. It is as beautiful and as spiritual as you get. I really love playing on that stage.

The Blues Brothers performed "Sweet Home Chicago" at every House of Blues, but Chi-Town is their hometown, and if there was anyplace to evoke the spirit of John Belushi, aka Joliet Jake Blues, it was in sweet home Chicago. And that's where Jim Belushi, aka Zee Blues, looked up to the boxes and sang, "One and one is two, two and two is four, I see my brother Jake walking through that door!" And the crowd screamed as if they'd all seen the glowing visage of Jake Blues. Their performance on opening night went out live over the Internet and was recorded for posterity for a House of Blues Records release.

JIM BELUSHI: I've been saying that every time I sing for the last seventeen years. It's just a dedication I do to John at the end of the show. We also dedicate "She Caught the Katy" and "Soul Man" to Jake Blues.

ABOVE: (Left to right) John Goodman, Dan Aykroyd, Junior Wells, and Jim Belushi performing at the HOB Chicago groundbreaking.

MYRTLE BEACH (May 1997)

And then there's Myrtle Beach, South Carolina, which opened in 1997 to the sounds of Southern rock survivors 38 Special and Lynyrd Skynyrd. Situated along the White Point Swatch stretch of the coast, it may have once been a hideaway for notorious pirates like Blackbeard and Anne Bonney. Unlike at other venues, where Tigrett had to adapt his vision to the existing location, in Myrtle Beach he was free to build a Southern farmhouse for dining, with an adjoining tobacco barn that would serve as the music hall. The property even had its own gator farm. There were a couple of soft openings with Eric Johnson and Buddy Guy on May 2 and 3, 1997, but on May 4 the Blues Brothers, featuring Dan Aykroyd, Jim Belushi, and John Goodman, officially kicked off the night, with Travis Tritt and Jeff "Skunk" Baxter sitting in. And—true to what was fast becoming a treasured pastime for Dan Aykroyd—James Brown took the stage to wrap up the grand opening.

ISAAC TIGRETT: Myrtle Beach was the location where I felt we finally got it down: I designed that one, and it was the most beautiful of them all. It had the biggest showroom and the best back stage, technically speaking. We also started to do one or two dance nights because there was a local demand for it, and they were very successful, so that was really cool.

MICHAEL GROZIER: Isaac would show up before the opening of each venue to fine-tune things, make sure everything was right, and give the workers a pep talk about the philosophy of the company. He'd say, "I don't believe spirituality is practiced on Saturdays and Sundays through some ceremony. I believe it should be practiced every waking moment. Thought, word, and deed must be the same thing. If you're saying one thing and doing something else, you're wasting time and wasting life."

ISAAC TIGRETT: Here's a funny story for you: The mayor of Myrtle Beach was part of the KKK, and after Dan Aykroyd rode with James Brown on the back of his motorcycle, they got off and took a photo with him. Imagine the picture of the KKK mayor with his arm around James Brown! I couldn't believe it!

Once again, House of Blues provided a comfy mattress for strange bedfellows. What a sight: the black soul singer who emerged from the civil rights struggle in the South arm in arm with a KKK mayor who, no doubt, was trying to come correct after being on the wrong side of history.

OPPOSITE: Guitar slinger David Navarro performing at HOB Myrtle Beach. **ABOVE:** HOB Myrtle Beach is a vibey venue with a Southern-style farmhouse built for dining and a tobacco barn for a concert hall, all surrounded by a former gator farm.

KEN JORDAN: We just love House of Blues in Orlando.

SCOTT KIRKLAND: The Orlando venue really hired the right people, including security, who knew the scene. We were impressed that a big company with many locations like House of Blues could have such individual focus on that crowd. It's one of the many reasons they're so successful.

KEN JORDAN: The House is on Disney property, so I got to see a Cirque du Soleil show before one of our gigs. And our gigs there always get a really great crowd. [When we went] down to Florida for the Winter Music Conference, there was a radio station that gave us a lot of support. We ended up doing a show with Fatboy Slim at House of Blues.

SCOTT KIRKLAND: The summer of 2001 we were on a tour for our second album, *Tweekend*, and it was a pretty big tour. We did some stuff with MTV and were down in Orlando for a big sold-out show. We were playing "Keep Hope Alive," [which has] a big build in the song, and I decided to stand on top of my X stand with my keyboard in my hand and sort of thrust the keyboard as I played the part over my head in some sort of ridiculous heavy metal pose from a long-gone era. I had my left leg anchored in the X stand, and my other leg on top of the keyboard, and I decided to do something I never did before—throw the keyboard as high up in the air as I could while I got back on the floor and watch it crash back down onto the X stand, where I would continue to play it—if it wasn't broken. I went to jump back down and my leg got stuck in the stand. My whole body went backward, and my kneecap completely popped out. I had so much adrenaline running in me I was trying to tell myself, "Oh, no, no, this doesn't hurt, it's okay." They took me back to the paramedics, who said, "You know, you really should go to the hospital." But the crowd was out there chanting, a really great crowd. My wife was yelling, "Don't cut his jeans, I just bought him those jeans!" I asked if it was going to get any worse. They said, no, but it would swell up. So I changed into shorts, went back out there, sat on a chair, and finished the set.

ORLANDO (September 1997)

After Isaac Tigrett floored the Disney execs in Los Angeles with the Jake and Elwood bars, they saw a future collaboration between House of Blues and the Mouse. It came to fruition in 1997 when House of Blues opened up in Downtown Disney's west side. Along with its juke joint vibe, the Florida property features a 100-foot-tall water tower that Tigrett spotted on a train ride through the Midwest and is now a landmark on the Downtown Disney promenade. Along with the traditional "Crazy Quilt" is Mr. Imagination's Unity Arch, reinforcing, once again, the all-inclusive philosophy of House of Blues. A Blues Brothers set worthy of "Bob's Country Bunker" kicked off the soft opening, as did Cypress Hill, who rapped about the "chronic" and no doubt made Minnie Mouse shake in her skirt.

MICHAEL GROZIER: We lost money at the Olympics because we weren't ready to go public yet, even though Atlanta was one of the most successful clubs we had. So now we were getting together with Disney.

If Mickey and Minnie Mouse were a bit nervous with the hip-hop and the heavy metal, at least they loved to dance. Orlando has long been a sanctuary for electronic beats and the glow-stick set, and House of Blues Orlando would be no different. The venue turned out to be a great place to rave, a phenomenon Scott Kirkland and Ken Jordan of the Crystal Method experienced firsthand.

ABOVE: A standout feature of HOB Orlando is its 100-foot-tall water tower, which Tigrett spotted on a train ride through the Midwest and later acquired.

LAS VEGAS (March 1999)

When House of Blues hit the Las Vegas strip it immediately became a destination, and it stands today as a fan and musician favorite. Located inside the Mandalay Bay Hotel & Casino, the venue maintains its humble juke joint vibe but pays tribute to its place among the high rollers with a beautiful chandelier from Kirk Kerkorian's old MGM hotel that hangs above the crowd during every show. The Blues Brothers didn't just open the club; they opened the hotel as Dan Aykroyd, Jim Belushi, and John Goodman led a parade of Harley-Davidsons up the strip and through the doors of the Mandalay Bay on opening day. They may call it Sin City, and on the opening night of March 2, 1999, Bob Dylan did perform the Grateful Dead's "Friend of the Devil," but he was "Knockin' on Heaven's Door" when, according to Rolling Stone's Roger Smith, U2's Bono "walked on, grabbed a six-string, and freestyled a bit: 'Here we are in the House of Blues / Black tie and cowboy shoes / Not much to win but a whole lot to lose / Feel like I'm knockin' on heaven's door.'" Black tie and cowboy shoes, huh? That about says it all.

DAN AYKROYD: Every House of Blues we opened had a memorable opening night, but I particularly remember going to see Bob Dylan that night with Bono, and yeah, it was incredible.

ARICH BERGHAMMER: Las Vegas was the first time that one of our venues was completely disconnected from the Foundation Room. You have the casino, the restaurant, and the club on one side, and the venue and Foundation Room on the other side. Around the time of the opening, the hotel floor had settled and dropped about eighteen inches, so it was off kilter. To make matters worse, the day before we opened, the hotel was putting in a wave machine, which leaked and ended up filling our whole floor with sand and water. They had to rip up the flooring and lay down temporary carpet in order to open

up that night. We also had our own House of Blues floor inside the Mandalay Bay Hotel, which really looked like a House of Blues hotel and was really cool.

LONN FRIEND: I'll tell you where my favorite House of Blues is right now: Las Vegas. I think it's the best room in Vegas. I saw so many great shows there, like Porcupine Tree, in front of four hundred people. Five years later they were playing Radio City Music Hall and selling out six-thousand-seat venues with no opening act. The greatest thing about House of Blues in Las Vegas is that they built a private VIP balcony that looks right down onto the stage. It's on the left of the stage, and the first time I got the experience was to see Joe Satriani. His manager put me there, and it was so much fun because you're literally hovering over the stage looking down and covering the concert like you're in a mini-blimp. It's so badass! It took some vision to build that kind of thing.

DAVE KING of Flogging Molly: I'm not a gambling man by any stretch of the imagination, but I remember that show we did with John Prine. We had to go upstairs in the casino area for a second. I had a quarter and I put it into the slot machine, and it gave me another quarter. So I put that quarter back in and then it wouldn't work. Then I noticed that the light was flashing on the machine. A guy comes over and says, "Oh, man, that's a bummer." I said, "What do you mean?" He said, "You only put a quarter in, didn't you?" I go, "It's all I had." He said, "Well, you just won $800 on a quarter." I would have won ten grand. But anyway, I got the $800 and I went back into the Foundation Room and bought everybody a drink.

CARLOS SANTANA: When I play at my residency at House of Blues Las Vegas, I just close my eyes and I could be in Woodstock or Carnegie Hall, you know? It's just pure music, and at that moment, House of Blues becomes the heart of Las Vegas.

ABOVE: View of the Strip from the Foundation Room at HOB Las Vegas. **OPPOSITE:** Carlos Santana performing at HOB Las Vegas.

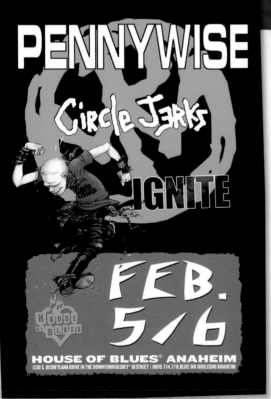

ANAHEIM (January 2001)

Not to be outdone by Los Angeles, with its physical and folkloric tributes to the Crossroads, is a juke joint from another world, or rather, another land—Disneyland.

French doors from New Orleans flank its Rose Terrace, and it's painted to reflect heaven, Earth, and the temptations to be found down at the Crossroads. And then there is the music. The first month was jam-packed with an assortment of local heroes and international headliners: Big Sandy and His Fly Rite Boys, followed by Lit, blues legend John Lee Hooker, a hip-hop night with Jurassic 5 and Supernatural, Latino act Jaguares, and rock-steady reggae artist Gregory Isaacs. Guitar wizard Steve Vai also had a huge opening night in Anaheim, which was followed by a week of Social Distortion, whose consecutive nights were broken only for a performance by Nikka Costa.

For Kevin Morrow, the key to success for booking Anaheim and other venues was to disregard the fair-weather tourists and concentrate on making the locals happy. "Appealing to locals is the way all House of Blues venues have succeeded. It will be just like the one in Orlando. Ninety percent of the concert traffic there is local. We don't have tourists coming in months in advance for a show they don't even know exists. The emphasis is always at the local level," he told Ben Wener of the Orange County Register just a few days before the opening night in 2001.

HOUSE of BLUES® ANAHEIM

1530 S. DISNEYLAND DRIVE IN THE DOWNTOWN DISNEY® DISTRICT
INFO: 714.778.BLUE® or HOB.COM/ANAHEIM

BAD BRAINS

SPECIAL GUEST
WHOLE WHEAT BREAD

Tuesday **SEPTEMBER 25**

HOUSE ☆ BLUES.   Produced by LIVE NATION

Make no mistake, House of Blues Anaheim may be in Downtown Disney, but it is no Mickey Mouse Club. Things got off to a raucous start, perhaps too wild, and the Mouse wasn't too fond of the rabid fans who showed up for some hard-hitting punk and metal shows.

MICHAEL GROZIER: It's a cool little pillbox, plantation-looking front, and it's got a rocking club. I think it is one of the greatest rock rooms we've had, though recently Disney applied some guardrails. A lot of the heavy metal and mosh-pit acts don't play there anymore.

ARICH BERGHAMMER: I would say that Anaheim was Disney-ized, because we had to come from a place of being cool to people who were not so cool. You wanted to be cool but tempered cool, which was completely different than Las Vegas. I remember standing up above with an executive at Disney saying, "You see riot, I see fun. You see out of control, I see a culture."

"YOU SEE RIOT, I SEE FUN. YOU SEE OUT OF CONTROL, I SEE A CULTURE."
—*ARICH BERGHAMMER*

BELOW: House of Blues Anaheim is perhaps the edgiest joint in Downtown Disney and frequently books local punk rock legends such as Social Distortion, whose front man, Mike Ness, is pictured here.

ANJALI RAVAL: What's really, really important for us when we open a venue is to make sure that the local community feels welcome and that we are welcomed by the local community. That's key. So when we open a new venue we find a way to make sure that there is a local angle tied to it—officials, dignitaries, or a local charity from the area. When we opened up Anaheim we had Lit, a punk rock band from Orange County, and then we had Social Distortion, also from the Anaheim area.

JEREMY POPOFF of Lit (as told to *The Orange County Register*): The first time we played a House of Blues, we were nobody. I think we were opening for Eve 6 and had probably sold twenty thousand records. But they treated us like real stars. It was awesome to have fully stocked dressing rooms, complete with clean towels and soap. They treat the bands with a lot of respect.

CLEVELAND (November 2004)

What better place for an old rusty juke joint but in the buckle of the Rust Belt: Cleveland, Ohio? Simply stated, "Cleveland Rocks!" It's where disc jockey Alan "Payola" Freed talked over the blues, country, and R & B and hyped a hybrid of these sounds he coined "rock and roll." It's where the Rock and Roll Hall of Fame sits in recognition and celebration of what Cleveland has brought to the party, and it's where House of Blues opened up a new juke joint inside an old Woolworth building in 2004. With a whopping 47,000 square feet of concert and dining space, the venue features works by local artist Peter Wood and ironwork throughout to honor the city's manufacturing history. The choice of opening act was also carefully calculated. What better way to celebrate the rejuvenation of Cleveland than to reunite its most beloved band, power-pop perfectionists the Raspberries? It was nothing short of Raspberriesmania, or, as Michael David Toth of the Cleveland Free Times *reported, "Friday's first live appearance of all four original Raspberries in over three decades was one of the biggest local music events of recent memory, with an estimated half of the sold-out tickets plucked by out-of-towners from as far away as Japan." Ken Sharp, author of two books on the power-pop icons (*Overnight Sensation: The Story of the Raspberries *and* Raspberries Tonight!*) was one of those rabid fans who flew in for the special occasion.*

ABOVE: Lead vocalist, rhythm guitarist, and pianist for the Raspberries, Eric Carmen called the reunion show at HOB Cleveland "the most fun [he] had ever had onstage." **OPPOSITE:** The vibrant House of Blues in Cleveland played a major role in the revitalization of the downtown area. It, along with the nearby Rock and Roll Hall of Fame, makes Cleveland an unassumingly rockin' city.

KEN SHARP: For many years, the chances of the Raspberries reuniting was slimmer than a sumo wrestler tipping the scales under two hundred pounds. But in 2004 the improbable happened; the Raspberries were reuniting to perform a special show at the newly opened House of Blues in the band's hometown of Cleveland. Plane ticket in hand, I made the trek from Los Angeles to Cleveland and arrived a day early out of worry that an unexpected travel snafu could derail my trip. When the curtains opened to the joyous Rickenbacker-powered sounds of "I Wanna Be with You" filling the beautiful new venue, I had a smile on myself bigger than the Empire State Building. I was finally seeing the Raspberries live in concert, hearing them perform kick-ass versions of such songs as "Tonight," "Ecstasy," "Go All the Way," and "Overnight Sensation." It blew my mind—LSD not required!

Cleveland native and House of Blues booker Anthony Nicolaidis spoke to Ken Sharp for his book Raspberries Tonight!

ANTHONY NICOLAIDIS (as told to Ken Sharp): The company had decided that we had a certain amount of money to spend on talent to open up the House of Blues in Cleveland. They felt that it had to be dramatic. It had to be big. We've opened up these clubs in the past with acts like Aerosmith. But since I'm from Cleveland, I thought, "What would be more dramatic than a Raspberries reunion?" My direct supervisor, Bob Shea [vice president, House of Blues concerts], grew up with the Raspberries, and when I told him, he said, "Oh man, that would be great. Go for it!" I honestly didn't think it was possible. I didn't think it could

happen. But it was worth a shot. What's the worst they could say? No? After talking with Jim, he agreed to have me meet Eric to discuss the idea. And as I drove out to Eric's house, a scene from *The Blues Brothers* flashed in my mind. It was that scene where the Blues Brothers said, "We want to put the band back together. We're on a mission from God." That's kind of how I felt. Like I was on a mission from God.

ERIC CARMEN (as told to Ken Sharp): It was just mind-boggling. When I talked to the Cleveland House of Blues people about our first show, and they told me that 50 percent of the tickets were sold to out-of-towners, I said, "What do you mean?" Half of the people at our first reunion show came from somewhere else. They weren't natives. That was pretty astonishing. We have some very special and devoted fans who've followed this band and stayed with us all this time. After the show, I was completely exhausted. In fact, I don't know when I'd ever been so exhausted—just emotionally drained. It was the most fun I've ever had onstage. To put this band back together and have Wally standing there on my left doing those guitar parts that I haven't listened to or played since 1973 was great! We were overwhelmed by the crowd's reaction to that first show at House of Blues.

The Cleveland opening was also Arich Berghammer's baby, and he told the Cleveland Plain Dealer *that the club threw the party "as a big thank-you to everyone who helped it open."*

ARICH BERGHAMMER: We were an anchor brought into a struggling community. I'll never forget the taxi ride I took to the location six

months before it opened. The driver was like, "You're not getting off here, are you?" I said, "This is the correct address, right?" But he insisted, "No, let me take you to your hotel. You don't want to get out here." I told him not to worry, and he told me I was nuts.

We never had so many people show up to a job fair looking for work, either, some of them with their kids on the line, looking like they hadn't worked in years. I told our people, "I don't care if it takes all night into the next day, we're going to give each and every one of them the proper respect and interview them." Some of those people are still working there today. My biggest takeaway was that the venue was the heartbeat for the redevelopment of downtown Cleveland.

The proximity to the Rock and Roll Hall of Fame, though the museum is confined to its own grounds, isn't forgotten by anyone, especially two Cleveland cousins and bona fide Rock and Roll Hall of Fame members, Michael "Kidd Funkadelic" Hampton and Lige Curry, guitarist and bassist for George Clinton's P-Funk.

MICHAEL "KIDD FUNKADELIC" HAMPTON: We feel at home at every House of Blues, but especially the one in Cleveland. We get some dinner, we get some drinks, we run into people from all

walks of life, as well as some old familiar faces. I always try to do my best there. It's easy in Cleveland because I can channel the energy that I get from my hometown crowd.

LIGE CURRY: House of Blues Cleveland coincided with the whole area of downtown that they were trying to bring up. It's beautiful, man. In the middle of the show George introduced Michael and me and explained how he ran into us in Cleveland when I was just sixteen and Michael was seventeen! I think the Rock and Roll Hall of Fame and House of Blues is a great match for Cleveland, because Alan Freed was from Cleveland and he was the first one to play Chuck Berry, Little Richard, and Bo Diddley when other stations wouldn't.

ARICH BERGHAMMER: There's something really incredible about the connection between P-Funk and Cleveland. You will never find a more proud community, and you won't understand that until you see them come out to watch P-Funk. People come out who were friends with them since they were kids, generations of fans that come to support this band. There's not that much depth and tradition in Los Angeles, but Cleveland has insane tradition.

"CLEVELAND HAS INSANE TRADITION."
—ARICH BERGHAMMER

SAN DIEGO (May 2005)

One can assume that a surf shack may be more appropriate than a juke joint for the beach town that is San Diego. But San Diego is a community with a vibrant music scene and a diverse populace that loves to party, and there couldn't be a better spot for its House of Blues than in the heart of the historic Gaslamp District. Located in the old Woolworth building, the venue also has a sidewalk café for those who love to stroll. The Wailers kicked things off, and George Clinton was in the house the very next night, followed by Ozomatli with Damian "Jr. Gong" Marley, desert rockers Queens of the Stone Age, some OG punk with Bad Religion, and the Blues Brothers with John Mayall, and the month closed out with goth crooner Peter Murphy. If that wasn't enough, Diamond Dave, aka David Lee Roth, and his band brought some vintage Sunset Strip to San Diego for a party people are still talking about.

OPPOSITE: The dining room concert hall at HOB San Diego is a favorite for locals and local musicians alike. Pictured is San Diego rockabilly and blues group The Jerry "Hot Rod" Demink Band. **ABOVE:** Like HOB Cleveland, HOB San Diego is a lively hub in what was for a time a less-than-inviting neighborhood. Today San Diego's Gaslamp District is a hotbed of music and culture.

ANJALI RAVAL: I remember that week of openings in San Diego with Damian Marley as being very conducive to San Diego. I remember having tons of college students there, since we give discounts for students of Cal State San Diego and U.C. San Diego. They love their Latin rock in San Diego, too. It's a very youthful demographic.

DAN AYKROYD: The opening of San Diego was just a stunning week of music.

MICHAEL GROZIER: We had a lot of great shows there. I remember David Lee Roth and the Blues Brothers and a lot of important people from the San Diego community. Mostly I recall everything just running smoothly.

ARICH BERGHAMMER: Dan was very close with people in the military, and I remember getting the approval for him to ride his motorcycle off an aircraft carrier and ride all the way through downtown and up to the club, where Deepak Chopra was standing with Dan's wife, Donna Dixon. I remember putting aside around three hundred tickets for any last-minute VIPs, and I got advice from David Cone—considered *the* man in the Gaslamp District—who told me exactly who I needed to take care of. You never know who is going to show up last minute, and if we weren't able to get them through that night we could have very quickly ruined a boatload of relationships.

DALLAS (May 2007)

Dallas, Texas, gave us so much more than the Cowboys and the bad fictional oilman J. R. Ewing. Sister-city Fort Worth was where Bob Wills and Milton Brown formed the Light Crust Doughboys, and it's where they helped pioneer the Western swing sound. And while it wasn't recorded in Dallas, the song "Dallas Blues," by a German immigrant and fiddler, Hart Wand, is arguably the first genuine blues song published. "There's a place I know / folks won't pass me by / Dallas, Texas, that's the town / I cry / oh hear me cry / And I'm going back / going back to stay there til I die / until I die." House of Blues Dallas was opened in 2007 in the city's historic White Swan Building, an industrial coffee-roasting plant that was added to the National Register of Historic Places in 1978. The building may be old school, but when it comes to power it makes other properties green with envy, as House of Blues is powered by renewable energy from the Green Mountain Energy Company. Grand opening acts included Old 97's, Erykah Badu, Kings of Leon, Joss Stone, Live, and, of course, the Blues Brothers.

NIGEL SHANLEY: I came in as a consultant for six weeks for the opening of Dallas, which was wonderful because of the weather and because Dan led a big bike ride to the club. From a technical and a sound point of view, there's no better House of Blues than Dallas; it's beautiful, and it's a musician's house.

PAUL SHAFFER: Dallas was incredible for me because I got to play with Albert King and Chuck Berry. The Blues Brothers band backed up Albert King, and then Chuck Berry closed the evening. But Berry didn't want to play with the Blues Brothers because he likes to work with local bands he's never played with before. So after our set with Albert King, I was having a drink by the bar when someone came up to me and said, "Chuck Berry won't go on without you!" As surreal as it seems, I got to go back out onstage and played a set with Chuck Berry. It was a phenomenal, phenomenal night.

ABOVE: HOB Dallas is located in a repurposed coffee-roasting plant and has a high-ceilinged concert hall. **OPPOSITE:** Johnny "Clyde" Copeland performing at HOB Cambridge but, as always, repping Texas and the Lone Star State's contributions to the blues. **PAGES 68–69:** West London new folk group Mumford & Sons performing at HOB Dallas.

Jo Bo'

Break a leg Tonight—
Paul and his band will
open with 'House Is A
Rockin'' and close with
'Purple Haze'. Remember he
did this in Vegas and ripped
the roof off the place.
It will set us up nicely.
Also let's add 'Driving
Wheel' to our running order

Thanks
DEL   AT/1hr
               DIRECTS
               HOB

               OPENING

HOUSTON (October 2008)

Houston, Texas, has its own connection to the blues. This was the home of Don Robey's Peacock Records, where Big Mama Thornton recorded "Hound Dog" in 1953. Houston is also the home of ZZ Top, the trio that took the blues, the Texas boogie, some long beards, and a pair of "Cheap Sunglasses" and became one of the state's most popular exports. The venue was built from scratch, and it's also the anchor of the Houston Pavilions outdoor shopping and entertainment complex—they christened it the Bronze Peacock Room as a tribute to the label and the first club where Big Mama Thornton and Lightnin' Hopkins played. The opening month went from the requisite Blues Brothers performance to rap mogul Jay-Z and special guest DJ AM, who had survived a plane crash the month before. The Houston Chronicle's Joey Guerra reported: "It was, to say the least, a scene. Sharp-dressed men in suits mingled with others in ball caps. Girls in Saturday night outfits nibbled pizza on plastic plates. And a gaggle of Houston Texans players— including Mario Williams, Anthony Weaver and Travis Johnson—partied in a roped-off section."

SCOTT KIRKLAND: Yeah, Houston is a really good House of Blues. It's got a great crowd, and they really pay attention to detail over there.

KEN JORDAN: There's not one person who didn't appreciate the night we played House of Blues Houston. It's a big room, and again, the hospitality and the food were second to none.

RINGO STARR: A major hero of mine was Lightnin' Hopkins. I loved the blues. You know, life is weird: When I was eighteen I went to the American consulate in Liverpool with a friend of mine because we wanted to move to Houston, Texas, because Lightnin' was from there. I worked at a factory at the time and we were looking for factory jobs in Houston, and we went to the embassy and they gave us all these forms to fill out, and we filled them out and we after we filled them out there was more forms. Well, we were eighteen, and we didn't go, but life is a strange path and we're just on it. It would have been interesting if I had immigrated to Houston: what would have happened? Would I have been playing the blues instead?

ABOVE LEFT: ZZ Top's blues and Texas boogie guitar wizard Billy Gibbons. **TOP:** Scott Guion's HOB Houston mural pays homage to Texas blues legends Johnny "Guitar" Watson, Big Mama Thornton, Lightnin' Hopkins, and Albert Collins.

BOSTON (February 2009)

When the Cambridge House of Blues finally closed its doors in 2003, there was an immediate void. The club had become a fixture in the scene and was beloved for its intimacy, but, frankly, it was too small. So how would House of Blues compensate for the loss of such a Beantown landmark? Easy: Open a much bigger House of Blues across the street from the ultimate Boston landmark institution, Fenway Park. Almost ten times the size of the original location, with a service capacity of almost 2,500 guests and a staff of 200 to cater to them, the new and improved House of Blues has a stage and a sound system that not only makes electric guitars sound more electric but also is suitable for today's paparazzi-magnet pop stars, like Lady Gaga and Katy Perry—both of whom snapped, crackled, and popped on its stage, pyrotechnics and all.

Rituals from House of Blues past were honored—the "Mississippi Mud Pour," the "Crazy Quilt," and the Gospel Brunch—but the venue also honors its collegiate Cambridge House by offering up-and-coming and local acts a smaller stage, closer in size to the original House of Blues. The artists who opened the first month were also worthy of the diverse audience the club caters to. The Gypsy Kings, B.B. King and Buddy Guy, the Disco Biscuits, Flogging Molly, electro-house act Cut Copy, Jay-Z, Willie Nelson, TV on the Radio, Rick Springfield, George Clinton, and P-Funk are just some of the acts that appeared on the calendar. And, as usual, no opening would be complete without a performance by Dan Aykroyd, Jim Belushi, and the Blues Brothers, backed by the Sacred Hearts band.

MICHAEL GROZIER: Now we're in the old Pat Lyons building, where nightclubs like Axis and Avalon once were, and there's much more room to do what we really do best, which is entertain a lot of people. It's right outside Fenway Park, and looking at it is like "Wow! We've made that transition from a two-hundred-person place to the two-thousand-seat venues that we have today.

FRANKIE "KASH" WADDY: We helped open Boston. I love that venue. It's the biggest, and it's a killer place. You come out of the dressing room, make a left turn, then a right turn, and you're right onstage. I've got killer photos from opening night. I remember Dan Aykroyd was there, and to hype up the crowd before our set I came onstage and yelled at the crowd, "Is this the city of the Boston Tea Party?" And they yelled back, "Yeah! Yeah!" I said, "Well, tonight, it's the Boston 'P' Party!" I think it ended up in a quote somewhere because they loved it at the club, so they used it.

In twenty years, House of Blues opened thirteen one-of-a-kind venues, each mindful of its own unique style while sharing values in design, food, art, and, most of all, music.

TOP RIGHT: HOB Boston sits across the street from Fenway Park. With a capacity of nearly 2,500, the venue has gone a long way toward filling the void left in the music scene by the closure of HOB Cambridge in 2003. **PAGES 72–73:** Buddy Guy performing at HOB L.A. during its 10th Anniversary celebration.

chapter three

CROSSROADS OF MUSIC:
HOUSE OF BLUES TO "PLANET ROCK"

It may be called House of Blues, and its roots may tap to the tunes that arose at the Crossroads of Highways 61 and 49, but with an *ALL IS ONE* ethos welcoming tastes of every persuasion, the venues soon boasted a diversity of musical styles. Which made sense, especially when considering the fact that blues is the foundation and inspiration for more modern music than most imagine. Isaac Tigrett, Teo Leyasmeyer, and Kevin Morrow figured out pretty early that they had to book acts of every flavor in order to satisfy the diverse palate of the Cambridge House clientele. Their eclectic programming and extraordinary sound and staging created an environment where fans could experience their favorite music and musicians in the best conditions possible—intimate, atmospheric, and sonically dynamic enough to stun even the most passionate audiophile.

KEVIN MORROW: I told Isaac, "We really need to do hip-hop, we need to do metal, we need to do folk—we need to be doing everything." We agreed that on any given night we should have a completely different fan base in House of Blues.

Morrow assembled a team of trusted bookers across all locations, and their success didn't go unnoticed.

KEVIN MORROW: I gotta tell you, as cool as it was to win those Pollstar awards, it was even cooler to watch the guys I hired win the awards after me—every guy I hired ended up winning Pollstar Talent Buyer of the Year. Go back to the golden era of House of Blues and you'll see Sonny Schneidau, Mike Krebs, Michael Yerke, and Sean Streigal. Every year it was another House of Blues

guy. There was a time when *Billboard* magazine put out the Top Twenty Clubs, and we were nine of the top eleven in tickets sold. We put together an amazing team, and winning those awards was fun for me, but as an ex–basketball player, it became more fun making the assist than making the shot all the time.

ANJALI RAVAL: One of the most exciting things about House of Blues is that we feature a wide spectrum of musical genres on our stages on any given week. One night, you can see a heavy metal band, followed by a reggae artist the following night, followed by a gospel choir or ensemble on Sunday afternoon. I think that was always Isaac's vision: to house artists from every genre under one roof and on the same stage, night after night.

OPPOSITE: Bo Diddley performing at HOB L.A. on January 2, 2004. Bo Diddley's influence on rock-and-roll artists such as Jimi Hendrix and the Rolling Stones makes him a perfect example of the HOB ethos, which celebrates the influence of blues on modern music.

MICHAEL FRANTI: One night it could be somebody playing really authentic roots music and the next night it could be an incredible techno DJ, on another night you can have a heavy metal band playing there, while on Sunday you have gospel. The diversity of music at House of Blues is the same diversity that makes the planet beautiful, and it's really important that we honor those roots and also honor the next generation of people who are breaking those boundaries. House of Blues does that really well.

By the mid-1990s, hip-hop was already big business. N.W.A was telling it like it was, but not everybody wanted to hear the message. They may have had no problem selling the records and counting the dollars, but fear of a rap planet and all the gang violence that threatened to come with it made booking hip-hop shows tough—even if the artist flowed about daisies over jazz breaks.

Arich Berghammer, executive VP for clubs and theaters, North America, for Live Nation, was the general manager of House of Blues on the Sunset Strip when the hip-hop explosion was taking off. It was often his job to make nice with the city officials who weren't so excited about the prospects of posses rolling into West Hollywood.

ARICH BERGHAMMER: I have to tip my hat to Kevin Morrow for standing firm in regard to the diversity of the music when we started booking hip-hop—I mean, the city hated it.

KEVIN MORROW: I started out a classic rock geek, then I became a blues and jazz geek, and then I moved into the roots music scene, but then I recognized that hip-hop was the new urban blues. When hip-hop hit, all of a sudden I had five nights of the Fugees, seven nights of D'Angelo, the Roots, Missy Elliott, the Notorious B.I.G., Outkast—you name a group, and we had them. When we booked all the straight-up hip-hop acts it made us cool, and then the new up-and-coming artists like Linkin Park and 311—the white hip-hop/KROQ-style bands—wanted to play where their heroes had played, and they started coming to our venue. I booked most of those shows through Cara Lewis, who managed all the hip-hop acts at William Morris at the time, and I can't give her enough credit for helping House of Blues Los Angeles get off the ground. It's funny; were just talking about Eminem's first show at Los Angeles House of Blues.

ANJALI RAVAL: We definitely had Public Enemy at House of Blues, but one of the things that makes me proud is that many of these hip-hop groups had some of the earliest shows of their careers at House of Blues. I recall when Jay-Z first performed with Ja Rule on our stage. Jay came back years later and launched Rihanna, who also did one of her first shows at the venue. Outkast also did one of their first performances with us, as did Jurassic 5, the Roots, and Kanye West.

CHALI 2NA: I was at the first Eminem show he did at Los Angeles when "Slim Shady" was out, and I was there when A Tribe Called Quest did their last show before breaking up. I saw Jay-Z there; I mean, I saw a lot of people there—I was there for one of the last Run DMC shows ever! I can say that our band, Jurassic 5, was born in 1994, and to see all of the major hip-hop groups as well as the underground hip-hop groups playing House of Blues felt like an accomplishment. There was high status associated with House of Blues as soon as it opened, and everybody in the world of hip-hop wanted to play there.

OPPOSITE: LL Cool J performing at HOB L.A., February 2006. **ABOVE LEFT:** Flyer for Public Enemy show at HOB New Orleans advertising $.25 draft beer and free red beans!

Jurassic 5's ebullient baritone, Chali 2na, first performed at House of Blues not with J5 but as a member of Angelino stalwarts Ozomatli—a group that represented the very essence of HOB's belief in unity in diversity by combining rock, Latin, hip-hop, jazz, and other musical styles on one stage. Ozomatli had gone from the underground clubs to champions of the L.A. scene—and they considered their House of Blues gig nothing less than a triumph.

is the Troubadour, and we played the Troubadour. Then we played the Whisky A Go-Go, and that was like, "Oh my god! All these amazing bands were discovered here!" And so each venue was like another step up, and House of Blues was one of the higher steps, if not the highest, just because of its status within the club world in Los Angeles.

Some of the hip-hop acts that appeared at House of Blues bubbled up from the underground, while others went pop, but it was the likes of N.W.A, Dr. Dre and Snoop Dogg, and Tupac Shakur who helped take underground hip-hop to a whole 'nother level.

CHALI 2NA: Tupac was hot at the time, and all kinds of things were happening around him in his circle. But while that stuff was happening in hip-hop, I was on the other side of the fence of the thug, gangster thing. So for me it was like studying stocks. I would go to the gangster shows just to see what they were doing and if their shows were different than ours, because we were putting so much into our shows and I wanted to see who had a good show and who didn't.

CHALI 2NA: It was overwhelming at the time. We were playing around Los Angeles and conquering different venues, and each one was gratifying in its own way. We started at little hole-in-the-wall joints, then moved to the Ivar Theater, then the Dragonfly, and then it was like, OK, the next step

KEVIN MORROW: It comes up because there's video out there of Tupac's last performance, which was at House of Blues. Tupac was a good guy and was at the club a lot. One night the Fugees were playing and he came down the bottom of the driveway, where the VIPs enter, and there were probably forty or fifty Crips there. The

"IT MAY HAVE BEEN THE GREATEST SHOW IN THE HISTORY OF HIP-HOP. HALF THE CROWD WAS IN RED AND THE OTHER HALF WAS IN BLUE, BUT THERE WERE NO PROBLEMS."
—KEVIN MORROW

ABOVE LEFT: Snoop Dogg performing at HOB Atlantic City, May 27, 2011.
TOP RIGHT: Jurassic 5 baritone Chali 2na feeling out the crowd at HOB L.A.
OPPOSITE: Kanye West performing with John Legend, February 2005, HOB L.A.

police were afraid to move them. The police were there for us, but on the other hand, they were outnumbered. I took Tupac aside and said, "Bro, can you help me out here? Obviously there's a situation and the police are getting agitated." He said, "Yes, but if I help you, will you let me in?" I said, "Of course." So he ran over to them and said, "Listen, y'all gotta leave. The police up there are going to come down here and they're going to get crazy, and then my man isn't going to be able to put on any more hip-hop shows." And they all left.

problems, and I said, "Well, what about the Fourth of July?" It may have been the greatest show in the history of hip-hop. Half the crowd was in red and the other half was in blue, but there were no problems. I remember the girl that I was dating loved Tupac and he gave her his shirt.

CHALI 2NA: There was tension, yes, but because of that tension there were a lot of lessons to be learned. I just think that out of that time came another generation of hip-hop, and I'm grateful

A couple of months later Andre Farr approached me and said Suge Knight wants to do a Death Row show with Dr. Dre, Snoop Dogg and Tha Dogg Pound, Warren G, Ice Cube, and, of course, Tupac. He said that Suge wanted to show that he was a legitimate businessman and could pull off a concert of this magnitude without

for all of the people that took a chance with this new musical form. It was beautiful to have that outlet at that venue, man. When we did the Word of Mouth Tour with Jurassic 5, Dilated Peoples, the Beat Junkies, and Supernatural at House of Blues, it was one of the most amazing shows I think we ever had.

DEATH ROW RECORDS PRESENTS

LIVE IN CONCERT!

THURSDAY
JULY 4th

8:00
PM

DESIGN BY: ALLAN SHREM

HOUSE OF BLUES
8430 SUNSET BLVD
EST HOLLYWOOD

> ## "JUST GET THEM AND PUT THEM BACK IN THE CROWD, BECAUSE WE'RE NOT GOING TO THROW PEOPLE OUT OF THE BUILDING FOR MOSHING"
> —ARICH BERGHAMMER

Thrash metal, a gritty iteration of its heavy counterpart, is notorious for its mosh pits—something it got from its early development in the hardcore punk scene. But whereas hardcore punk acts and slam dancing were banned in places like the Whisky A Go-Go, Arich Berghammer tells us that House of Blues has maintained an open mind, as long as safety isn't compromised.

ARICH BERGHAMMER: We would stand up on the balcony and look down and see the circle of people go round and round, and I'd say to the crew, "Look, guys, you can't control this. It's part of the culture, so you've got to let it happen to a point." And when they were flinging one another over the barricade and up on the stage, I insisted, "Just get them and put them back in the crowd, because we're not going to throw people out of the building for moshing."

Metal maniacs were in for a special treat when on July 18, 2000, Metallica performed at House of Blues on the heels of their Summer Sanitarium Tour. Only the one thousand fans in the audience didn't know they were there to see Metallica, as their performance was part of the Blind Date contest sponsored by Miller Genuine Draft. Needless to say, the unsuspecting audience got a little more than just the High Life.

KEVIN MORROW: Metallica is the ultimate metal band, and what I remember about that Blind Date show is that it was so loud inside the club that even with my earplugs I came out of there with my ears ringing. You could actually feel it, like you feel the bass beats at a hip-hop show; you could feel the music coming at you and hitting your clothes in such a confined space.

LONN FRIEND: Joe Satriani's *Surfing with the Alien* was a game-changing six-string masterpiece. *RIP* covered it from its release, and I played the infectious title track on my syndicated radio show every week for a year. I saw Satch at House of Blues in Las Vegas just after the new bird's-eye VIP balcony opened. It was like floating above the wizard whilst he whipped his riffing staff. And there's Steve Vai. Steve Vai may not surf, but he plays guitar like an alien. Caught him at the Vegas House of Blues with Tony MacAlpine and Billy Sheehan, too. Vai's a visionary composer and entrepreneur of the ax who has shepherded so many young players into the music mix.

"STEVE VAI MAY NOT SURF, BUT HE PLAYS GUITAR LIKE AN ALIEN."
—*LONN FRIEND*

KEVIN MORROW: Les Paul was another guy that was really big with us. He became a close friend. For many of our openings we paired Les with Steve Vai. One tribute, I had Steve Vai, Dave Edmunds, Stephen Stills, Jeff "Skunk" Baxter, Jeff Healey, and Slash!

ARICH BERGHAMMER: Let me tell you, one night—at one of the tributes to Les Paul—Steve Vai was walking down the hallway. And who was walking up the hallway? Eddie Van Halen!

OPPOSITE TOP: Joe Satriani. **TOP LEFT:** Paul Stanley of Kiss on a solo tour. **ABOVE:** "Space" Ace Frehley of Kiss on a comeback tour. **BOTTOM LEFT:** Slash (left) and Joe Perry of Aerosmith.

There are kings, there are queens, and then there are divas—and House of Blues had the honor of hosting some of the greatest of their ilk.

ARICH BERGHAMMER: We did a lot of glitz and glamour with some of the male stars, but when you mention women like Etta James, Terri Nunn, Nelly Furtado, Alicia Keys, and Lauren Hill, I would say that the passion supporting them far outweighed the male artists. I would see the line outside and some people would be there for days.

And the way the female artists treated their fans was different as well; they would come out and talk to people—they gave their fans a lot of respect, and it was powerful to watch.

HOWARD STOVALL: I'll tell you one of my favorite moments from House of Blues. In 1999 the Blues Foundation did a salute to the women in blues, and we gave lifetime achievement awards to Ruth Brown, Koko Taylor, and Etta James. I'll never forget Etta's acceptance

speech. She said, "All these young girls talking about being a diva and they don't know what diva means. Ruth Brown is a diva, Bonnie Raitt is a diva, and Etta James is a diva. These young girls wouldn't know a diva from a beaver." And the place just went down. I laughed so hard.

SHEMEKIA COPELAND: It was an awesome night. I got up and performed and it was very cool. I remember being up there and being happy that I was there to honor those ladies—three of my favorite singers. They were very good to me, and Ruth Brown and Koko Taylor were especially so. They are the ladies that paved the way for me.

OPPOSITE: Etta James performing at HOB L.A. in 2004. James is known for a style that spanned multiple genres, including blues, R&B, soul, jazz, gospel, and even rock, earning her an induction into the Rock and Roll Hall of Fame in 1993. **ABOVE LEFT:** R&B and soul singer Macy Gray performing at HOB Anaheim in October 2010. **TOP:** Kelly Rowland, Beyoncé Knowles, and Michelle Williams of Destiny's Child performing at HOB L.A., September 2004. **ABOVE RIGHT:** Blues singer-songwriter and slide guitarist Bonnie Raitt performing at HOB L.A., February 2006.

GHOSTLAND OBSERVATORY

TOP: DJ and producer Flying Lotus (Steven Ellison) performing at HOB L.A. in 2013. Grand-nephew of Alice and John Coltrane, FlyLo has music in his blood, and his diverse sounds are a showcase of musicology meeting modern production.

OPPOSITE: Deadmau5 sporting his signature mask during a performance at HOB L.A.

IT'S WAY TOO EASY TO DISMISS electronic dance music *as soulless, automated beats, but, frankly, that's a cop-out. Yes, Auto-Tune, computer beats, glow sticks, and LED screens come to mind. A quick examination of where the music comes from reveals that techno originated in Motor City, and house in Chicago. Both were taking funk and northern soul into the future, in just the way that Muddy Waters did when he made the transition from acoustic to electric guitar and plugged into a nearly distorted amp. Trainspot the old-school cuts that the genre's pioneers have sampled, and you will see that the blues, soul, R&B, funk, dub reggae, and rock and roll are just as present as they are on rap records. Moby, for example, sampled Dennis Coffey (the first white guy to appear on* Soul Train, *followed by David Bowie), Bobby Byrd, Lyn Collins, James Brown, Michael Jackson, the Soul Searchers, and Bessie Jones, bringing his audience back to songs from 1959. Looks like an abundance of soul here.*

And drum'n'bass—a combination of hard-core techno, hip-hop, and dub reggae—derives its groove from the "Amen Break," a drum solo (also widely sampled by early hip-hop artists) performed by Gregory Cylvester Coleman of the '60s funk and soul group the Winstons in an aptly named tune, "Amen, Brother." Why aptly? Because the Winstons, those purveyors of groove and good faith, never pursued copyright, thus giving the world the freedom to explore the endless permutations of their timeless backbeat.

Producers living in UK Council Estates (the British equivalent of the projects where hip-hop was born in the States) would take the "Amen Break" and match it with a cappellas of soul divas, similar to what they heard on those Chicago house records from the '80s. Those soul divas were repeating vocal acrobatics they got from the African American gospel music that came from the same churches Isaac Tigrett grew up in. So don't let the word electronic *scare you, because even a synthetic heart can be sacred, and that's why House of Blues opened its heart to EDM. The Crystal Method were part of that first wave of electronic acts to make the transition from illegal raves to legitimate concerts, and when they decided to come in from the cold, they entered a House of Blues.*

SCOTT KIRKLAND: From the very first big tour we played at House of Blues, each show just kept getting better and better. They were way ahead of their time, you know, as far as understanding the club scene.

KEN JORDAN: On the first album, we had a sold-out show and House of Blues added a second show, and I think we sold out both shows the same night.

SCOTT KIRKLAND: I can't emphasize enough the fact that House of Blues always hires the right people. It's impressive. Everyone involved knows the scene—not just the bookers—and that makes the artists feel like they are part of something special and tells the audience they're at the right place for the show they're looking for.

Paul McGuigan is a talent buyer for House of Blues and is responsible for bringing in some of the most cutting-edge electronic acts this side of the Pond. As Pablo Hassan, McGuigan's nom de bass, he is a resident DJ in L.A.'s seminal dubstep crew, SMOG, and like all HOB talent buyers, he possesses an intimate understanding of the scene.

PAUL McGUIGAN: The Crystal Method were way ahead of the game. I mean, when "Busy Child" came out around 1997 you could go to any kind of club and someone would drop that tune—you'd hear it a couple times a night. The thing that made them comfortable about playing a more traditional venue was that at the end of the night they knew they were going to get paid; they didn't have to go looking around a warehouse to find the promoter. They knew the party wasn't going to get busted by the cops, and there wasn't going to be any "Sorry, you're not getting paid tonight. The party got broken up before you went on because we didn't have a permit." They knew when they got off the stage the cash would be waiting for them. House of Blues took the rock model, where the bands are taken care of properly, and moved it over to EDM. As far back as 1996 House of Blues started working with outside promoters who were established in the electronic music world. People may have found it strange in the beginning because it wasn't in a nightclub setting, but they saw that it wasn't about the bottle service or the LED screens—that it was literally a thousand people in the room all facing the stage and the DJ is really the star.

Around 2006 we started to realize there was something going on with dubstep. SMOG fully embraced it, and we brought over artists from the UK: labels like Dub Police and artists like Caspa and Subscape. To make it work we had to create an environment that really presented this music in the right way, so we reinforced the sound, and we brought in some extra sub cabinets to make the place really rumble—because if you don't feel the bass, you're missing half the tune. We knew we couldn't treat the sound like a rock show, because without those extra cabinets you wouldn't get that London experience, and we wanted those UK artists to feel like they were at home.

Every subgenre of electronic music has been represented, too, from the indie-electronic sounds of LCD Soundsystem to the electro-house of Steve Aoki and the sophisticated trip-hop of Thievery Corporation.

MICHAEL GROZIER: Daft Punk has played the venues as well. So this place that seems initially all about homegrown indigenous art and wood floors and everything else can actually bring the nightclub feel. You know, it might be a challenge to stay on your toes, but House of Blues always adapts and embraces new musical cultures as they emerge.

> # "IF YOU DON'T FEEL THE BASS, YOU'RE MISSING HALF THE TUNE."
> *—PAUL McGUIGAN*

HOMEGROWN AND HOUSE TRAINED

The '90s offered a musical explosion that saw the rise of hip-hop, various forms of metal, indie rock, and electronic music, and a definite return to roots music, often in the form of country, bluegrass, blues, jam bands, and the punk bands that played DIY versions of rock and roll, just faster and louder. And they all had an opportunity to take chances and come into their own at House of Blues.

One such group was Flogging Molly, the Celtic-punk band that has its roots in Dublin but found a home at House of Blues. Lead singer Dave King tells us about the special relationship between the venue and the band.

DAVE KING: I remember the first time Flogging Molly ever played a House of Blues, when we all had our day jobs and were working all over the place in L.A. I got a phone call from our drummer, George. He'd just had a phone call from a House of Blues in Las Vegas, where Shane MacGowan had to cancel a show, and he was playing with John Prine—was there any way we could fill in? And I'll never forget it—we all got on the plane and we were so late in getting there that all the people let us off the plane first so we could run into taxis and race to the club. We walked out of the taxis and right up on the stage. The curtains were closed, and I remember the incredible experience of watching them open to reveal the audience.

Then we started to play in House of Blues in Los Angeles, which was the biggest gig we had ever done on our own. We really appreciate that they take chances on young bands, because when we were first starting out we never thought we'd ever play places like House of Blues. Unfortunately, there're not many places for young bands to play live these days. A place like House of Blues is inspiring for young bands. It's a place to look forward to and tackle, and that's a good thing for music.

Drummer for iconic Orange County punk band Social Distortion, and bartender at House of Blues Anaheim, David Hidalgo Jr., and his bandmate, Jonny "2 Bags" Wickersham, also appreciated the transition from fan to performer at House of Blues.

DAVID HIDALGO: Ironically, the first time I performed at a House of Blues, I opened for Social Distortion. I was in a band called Los Villains, and we were asked to do a couple shows on their first of many House of Blues runs. We did Anaheim and L.A. as well. It was an amazing experience. I will always be thankful to the guys for that opportunity.

OPPOSITE: *Pain* is tattooed in plain sight on the strumming hand of punk rock crooner Mike Ness—confirmation that hard knocks make up the story of his life.
TOP: Dublin-born guitarist Dave King and fiddle player Bridget Regan of Celtic punk band Flogging Molly performing at the HOB 20th Anniversary celebration in L.A.

HOUSE OF BLUES SUPER BOWL PARTY

In whose house did you watch Super Bowl XXXI in 1997? Well, if you turned on the TV for halftime, then you were at House of Blues for the "Blues Brothers Bash." Building on the success that they had with their pre–pop-up at the '96 Olympics, House of Blues turned the halftime show into a Mardi Gras party straight out of its New Orleans location. Joining the Blues Brothers Bash (Dan Aykroyd, Jim Belushi, and John Goodman) were ZZ Top and James Brown. The set list was equally classic, opening up with "Everybody Needs Somebody to Love," followed by "Soul Man," "I Got You (I Feel Good)," "Tush," and "Legs," and then everyone joined in at the end for "Gimme Some Lovin'" by the Spencer Davis Group. With the musicians and all the dancers wearing black hats and shades, everybody and their mother was a Blues Brother that night! "You just can't believe how incredibly exciting it is to see a brand you helped create take over the Super Bowl like that, with dancers wearing hats, glasses, and Blues Brothers logos," says House of Blues' maven of booking, Kevin Morrow, with much satisfaction. "We chartered a 727 filled with Dan Aykroyd's crew, Belushi, House of Blues people, and food—and we had a party all the way there."

MOBILE HOME: HOUSE OF BLUES ON TOUR

Only House of Blues could find a way to hitch a juke joint to a tour bus and take the show on the road. And not just one tour bus—a caravan of buses. The Smokin' Grooves Tour, for example, was one of the most successful hip-hop, funk, and reggae revues to ever hit the road. It featured the dopest names this side of the Cannabis Cup and was dubbed the Black Lollapalooza. For three years straight the tour offered hip-hop acts that were on top of their game and on the top of the charts—like Nas, the Fugees, Cypress Hill, Public Enemy, Busta Rhymes—sharing the stage with Ziggy Marley, Michael Franti, Erykah Badu, and George Clinton and P-Funk. "Rap had gotten a bad rap, if you'll pardon the pun," Dave Fortin explains. "I know that Kevin Morrow and Cara Lewis knew acts that had a positive message. The idea was that you could bring five hip-hop acts together and have a really safe and incredible music experience. It was a pivotal moment in hip-hop because it was now okay to like Common and other artists who showed that hip-hop wasn't just street music but positive roots music that everyone could enjoy." Kevin Morrow agrees: "The first hip-hop tours that went out in the '80s were brutal, with big fights. We were the first to put on a tour with hip-hop and reggae and funk."

Before it was pressed on CD or reissued, Funkadelic's *Tales of Kidd Funkadelic*—which was named after the brand-new seventeen-year-old guitar prodigy who hopped up on the Mothership and joined the P-Funk family, Michael "Kidd Funkadelic" Hampton—became a treasured disc for crate-digging producers who would sample the funk out of it. The Smokin' Grooves Tour succeeded in presenting a lesson in the history of African American music by pairing a group that laid down the tunes with a group like A Tribe Called Quest, who lifted and repurposed the grooves for a new generation. "I remember the combination of artists—we were good together," Hampton says, "and it felt like a real festival, like a traveling Woodstock." Reflecting on the camaraderie and the partying, he continues, "We all hung out together in the tour buses, and I still had a little youth in me, so it was a little crazy. I was raging a lot out there. Sometimes you'd get out of the tour bus and there was such a haze of smoke it was like, 'Where's the stage at?' You had to wait for the smoke to clear to find the stage!"

House of Blues launched other successful tours as well: There was the Barnburner Tour, with Joe Cocker, Buddy Guy, the Fabulous Thunderbirds, and the Radiators; and then another national tour called the Highway 61 Tour—every bit as much an ethnomusicology lesson as it was an amazing show. Your teachers for the evening? Buddy Guy, the Blind Boys of Alabama, and Billy Boy Arnold—all touring through colleges across the country. Morrow remembers the concerted effort to make the tour about more than just a series of concert set lists; it was meant to be a historical road map of American music. "When I put together the Highway 61 Tour, I created a logo that showed Africa reconnected to South America," he says. "So when you looked [at the design], it looked like you came out of Africa and right into New Orleans. I had Highway 61 running down Mississippi and into the middle of Africa. It was really tracing the roots of what American music was, aside from the English, French, Spanish, and other European influences. It was about African beats, African chants, and field chants, and then it went into gospel, blues, the migration to Chicago, soul, and then rock. The tour was about the history of African American music and how House of Blues fit into it."

Featuring:

Cypress Hill
Ziggy Marley & the Melody Makers
Fugees
A Tribe Called Quest
Busta Rhymes
Spearhead

SMOKIN GROOVES 1997

HAVE BLUES WILL TRAVEL

HOUSE OF BLUES

BARNBURNER

1996 TOUR

Featuring

JOE COCKER
BUDDY GUY
THE FABULOUS THUNDERBIRDS

THE RADIATORS

THE GALES BROTHERS

SPONSORED BY: VH1 MUSIC FIRST

JONNY "2 BAGS" WICKERSHAM: Having seen so many shows at House of Blues in Hollywood, it was real nice to be able to play on that stage. It was right after I started playing with Social D., and we played Hollywood and Anaheim.

MICHAEL GROZIER: O.A.R., another band that got its first exposure at House of Blues, started as a bunch of kids from Ohio State, and I remember they played a show in Chicago one summer while they were still in school. They had enough fans in Illinois that came out to support them, and finally they were doing six or seven shows for us. We're a national organization booking the best available talent, all the time. The challenge is to continue to find the cutting-edge acts, and find them first.

ANJALI RAVAL: I distinctly remember when I first started working for the company in 1997, as the venue's publicist, I had to create these really simple calendars that listed our shows for the entire month. I remember always having to check the spelling: I-N-C-U-B-U-S, and thought, "Why would you ever call your band Incubus?" But I always managed to spell it correctly, thank God. It was a pretty amazing feeling knowing

these bands enjoyed playing our club just as much as we loved having them. They would always return whenever there was an opening slot available. Kings of Leon got paid around a hundred dollars for their first gig when they opened for another band. Jason Mraz did one of his early shows here, and I remember him singing in the corridor stairwell right outside my office. He told me that that specific stairwell had the best acoustics for his vocal warm-ups. Sweet! I had my own personal pre-show performance! In 2002 we were handed a couple of young singer-songwriters out on their first co-headliner tour. I remember being in the music hall (near the stage) during their soundcheck, and being blown away by both of them. They both possessed this incredible raw talent that was so genuine and untapped. I immediately called a friend of mine, an entertainment producer for a local TV station, and said, "You have to send a crew to cover these kids. The next time they come through our town, they will be playing at Greek Theatre or some other big venue." It was John Mayer and Norah Jones. And I was right; they pretty much toured the sheds after that, and eventually ended up in arenas.

ABOVE: Norah Jones performing at HOB L.A., April 2002.

All genres were welcomed at the door, but a funny thing happened on the way to House of Blues—cats started playing the blues again. Sure, some of them said they were in a jam band, while others called it garage rock, or indie rock, but the most honest among them went back to calling it the blues.

Bands were going unplugged, pulling out mandolins. Or, like Lenny Kravitz and Ben Harper, they started playing through vintage guitars and amps. It was getting so that a fat guy could wear a fishing vest and play the harp and have a hit. The retro vibe was in the air, but there can be no doubt that House of Blues provided the environment for musicians to return to the roots and create a whole new generation—a revival, if you will, of the blues masters. You heard Willie Dixon—"Bring It On Home!"

MICHAEL GROZIER: Isaac believed that at the turn of the century everybody looks back and tries to pull things from the culture that they want to bring forward, and he thought of the blues as the taproot of American culture and music and that it should and would be brought forward.

DAVE FORTIN: I made that connection when I was at House of Blues Cambridge and this guy Luther Allison was performing. Teo was like, "You gotta go see him, you just gotta go." So I sat in the back and watched this older man burn down the house with his guitar. My jaw dropped. He shredded for three hours straight, pouring sweat. If you're not really into the blues, you have this notion that it's kind of slower with simple chords, but this man was destroying it. For me, a guy more connected with Trey Anastasio from Phish, all of a sudden I was seeing the connectivity to this guy playing such explosive blues guitar. I was like, "Oh my God, there must be more musicians like this." Sure enough there were: from Ronnie Earle and Chris Duarte to Coco Montoya. These guys were masters of their skill set and bridged the gap from the music I liked. They revived an interest in exploring this genre of the blues. I think House of Blues did that.

As the brand got bigger, people started to pay more attention to the acts coming through the building—acts like "Monster" Mike Welch, Kenny Wayne Shepherd, Jonny Lang, and Derek Trucks. And we felt blessed because we were the place that they would come through.

ABOVE: The hugely influential John Lee Hooker. His "talking blues" style became a beloved trademark throughout his career, as did his driving, piano-style guitar rhythms.

SHEMEKIA COPELAND: House of Blues started doing a bunch of blues tours, too. That Highway 61 Tour was great. I opened up for Buddy Guy and Robert Cray!

ARICH BERGHAMMER: I got a call from Jacquie Tedesco [one of the original House of Blues bartenders]. She got me to the front door and explained, "There's this kid wants to come in and watch a show but he's got no shoes on." I took a look at him. He was a kid, like, "I'm not even supposed to be out" sort of kid. But I sensed something special about him and let him in. Two years later, he's Kenny Wayne Shepherd and I'm writing him a check for thousands of dollars! He said, "Thank you for letting me in," and I replied, "Thank me? No, thank you, it's an honor!"

DAVE FORTIN: One night we were supposed to do a Glen Phillips show, but he got laryngitis. The manager called Teo and said that we shouldn't cancel the show because the opener was big with the college kids and people will definitely show up. We figured we had nothing to lose if at least fifty people made it out. Well, a lot more than fifty people came, more like a couple of hundred—the opener was John Mayer. Teo also started booking artists from Fat Possum Records, with guys like R. L. Burnside, who had a raw, raw, gritty sound. And when you listen to the Black Keys, you can hear that that sound is having a revival again—there's a circular way of coming back around.

MELISSA ETHERIDGE: I still see those things coming—the return to the roots, which have never really gone away. My kids are teenagers now, and they know when they hear something real: they love the real guitars, they love the strings, and they love the blues. The roots of it aren't going anywhere—the expression changes, sure, and it's beautiful how we interpret it as time goes on—but the roots never change.

OPPOSITE: Kenny Wayne Shepherd performing at HOB Atlantic City, September 2005. **ABOVE:** R. L. Burnside performing at HOB Cambridge. He was known for his gritty Mississippi and Delta blues sound, but his collaborations with underground garage rocker Jon Spencer marked him as a crossover artist with wide-reaching appeal.

SUSAN TEDESCHI: Blues is an important American tradition that needs to have a venue. There are a lot of blues festivals, but there aren't a ton of clubs. And honestly, people love the blues, and it's not all down—that's one misconception: that it's going to be a bunch of sad songs, but actually it can really lift you up and pull you out of a depression. People didn't have technology, but they could sit home and get a wire and a nail and hammer it into a piece of wood and make an instrument and sit around and play. So people like John Lee Hooker, Son House, or Lightnin' Hopkins would play these singular lines while singing at the same time and telling a story. And then people got creative with it and the blues went in different directions, from the early days of Charlie Patton to Buddy Guy.

House of Blues was a breeding ground for the next generation of blues musicians; Mike Welch is a perfect example of that. Here was a young guitar phenomenon and he was, gosh, thirteen back then, and for me he was the start of seeing all the young kids like Kenny Wayne Shepherd and Derek [Trucks] and all these new guitar players that started to get more known. So it definitely was a great time to start up new artists, and I'm definitely influenced by that whole scene—it really changed my career, and it's when I started playing blues predominantly.

ROBBY KRIEGER: Oh yeah, I've played "Roadhouse Blues" in House of Blues, and it was very apropos. I played there many times, but the last time I played House of Blues was with Ray Manzarek (one of the last times I've played with him, as a matter of fact), as part of the Sunset Strip Festival. They had a tribute to the Doors and they had three or four guys that gave speeches, and one of them was Marilyn Manson, who said if it wasn't for the Doors he wouldn't have been in music—we don't know if that's a good thing or a bad thing!

TOP: Jerry Portnoy on the harp with blues guitarist and singer Jimmy Rogers, HOB Cambridge. **ABOVE LEFT:** Blues singer and guitarist Susan Tedeschi performing at HOB Cambridge. Her current endeavor, Tedeschi Trucks Band, is a marriage of her band and that of her husband, Derek Trucks. **OPPOSITE:** Mississippi-born blues guitarist Byther Smith delivering his signature gritty sound at HOB Cambridge.

NORWOOD FISHER of Fishbone: At the end of the day I have a lot of love and appreciation for House of Blues. It's a great place to kick it and see some amazing shows. Music was changing drastically in the '90s, but then House of Blues came along and supported the concept of the blues and live music—something that could have faded into the background, but they kept it alive. I was on a plane not too long ago and there was this young girl who must've been in high school and happened to be a singer in a blues band. She could have easily been trying to become the next Britney Spears, but she was singing the blues—I think the fact that there is an institution like House of Blues, coming up at the time it did, standing strong, and expanding, had something to do with that. It came through and filled a void and created something where there was nothing, and that we didn't even know we needed until it came along.

WAYNE KRAMER: Everything we do is the blues; the story we tell is the blues, even when I'm talking about a policeman beating up a kid or a trip to another planet—it's still the blues. Everything is still connected and nothing exists in a vacuum, it's all part of the mash-up of what came before. The way I look at it is like a bow and an arrow: When I pull the bow back, I'm reaching back into the past for power—from all that music that's important to me, like Archie Shepp, Motown, Chuck Berry, Willie Dixon, and B.B. King—but pulling that bow back gives me the power to shoot the music into the future.

OH WHAT A NIGHT!

We've all had that night—that night! No matter if we were there to see our all-time favorite artist or if we took a chance on a "Pick of the Week" that totally blew up and sold out after we got in. At the end of the night, we were there for two things, the M&Ms. Not the green things that were removed from Van Halen's dressing room candy bowl, but the music and memories. And we all have them. For some, it was that enchanted evening Mary J. Blige teamed up with Elton John, or the night Lenny Kravitz joined Bootsy Collins for a funky romp. For others, it was finding out that Metallica was their Blind Date.

ABOVE: Justin Timberlake performing at HOB L.A., June 2003. **OPPOSITE BOTTOM:** Stevie Wonder performing at HOB L.A. in 2004. **OPPOSITE TOP:** Bootsy Collins (left) with drummer Frankie "Kash" Waddy.

ANJALI RAVAL: There are so many nights I remember, but some of the best were when somebody unexpected jumped up onstage. Lenny Kravitz with Bootsy Collins, or when Kid Rock jumped onstage with ZZ Top—all really great moments in time. One of my favorites was when Stephen Marley was performing, and I got a call on the radio that Stevie Wonder had just arrived and wanted to check out the show. Naturally, I escorted him and a few friends through the doors and into the VIP section. He decided he'd prefer to be inside the barricade, right in front of the stage. We got him settled, and I alerted Stephen Marley's crew that Mr. Wonder was inside the barricade. The next thing I know, they were literally pulling Stevie onto the stage to perform "Could You Be Loved"—the same song he performed once with Bob Marley, except this time, he was performing it with Bob's sons, Stephen and Ziggy. I'm pretty sure Ben Harper jumped onstage for that same song. For me, that was one of the most magical nights I've ever witnessed. It was so organic—so perfect.

DR. JOHN: I remember when Bootsy Collins was playing, but I had to leave because it was too loud for me.

BOOTSY COLLINS: I remember hands flying, people standing up, jammin' to the funk. The air was loose, the vibe was tight, people were happily funked up and getting more funked up by the pound. I remember Lenny Kravitz coming to the stage once we hit the first song and I told him let's wait so it would be a big surprise when I called him out to join the funk assault. He reluctantly held himself back, but the funk was so tenacious and furious that night that no one in the building had stage fright. At the time Lenny told me that he felt the power of the funk onstage. For his own shows he was using new technology, which at the time was performing with no amps on the stage, but after that night Lenny said "funk," and next time I saw him he had almost as many amps on stage as I did. The funk not only has to be heard, it must be felt. If you want to play with the big dogs, get you some big speakers.

MICHAEL GROZIER: Clearly on the top of the list was Elton John doing a *VH1 Storytellers* in New Orleans. It was right after Princess Diana and Versace had been killed, and I think this was his first appearance since those tragedies. It's when he first started to sing new lyrics to "Candle in the Wind"—I'm getting goose bumps just talking about it, because it was such a huge thing to have him in the building—and then for it to be part of a TV show that went out, and that it was in New Orleans, was just incredible.

SONNY SCHNEIDAU: New Orleans opened in January of 1994, and by November we ended up with two nights of Bob Dylan—his first time playing a House of Blues. We also had three nights of Eric Clapton, who asked Clarence

"Gatemouth" Brown to be his special guest because he knew he was local and the show would have a local feel to it. Those five nights in one month were pretty special. Crazy story about Clapton was that there were so few tickets that went on sale for that show but there were so many people calling to buy tickets that the phone exchange of the entire area went down— the whole system shut down, all for 600 tickets for a guy that could sell out arenas.

Eric Clapton and Bob Dylan were House of Blues creator Isaac Tigrett's two favorite artists. On one fateful evening in November 1994 Clapton was playing the Los Angeles club at the same time that Bob Dylan hit the stage in New Orleans.

ISAAC TIGRETT: I'll never forget the night that we had Eric Clapton playing in L.A. and Bob Dylan playing in New Orleans. Michael Grozier arranged to have me called when each hit the stage. I had one ear listening to Eric Clapton and the other listening to Bob Dylan, and I thought both were gods.

NIGEL SHANLEY: Having Eric Clapton for those three days in L.A. was the most difficult and the most wonderful three days for me because in his contract he basically owned House of Blues. They closed the Foundation Room for him and put in a foosball table, and he said, "I don't want any VIP's, I don't want any stars, and it will only cost thirty-five dollars a ticket and people can only buy two tickets through Ticketmaster." So everybody that had my number, every star, was dying to get in and I didn't have one ticket to give them. So one day I reintroduced myself to Clapton, who is God to me, and he said, "I understand you have all these people phoning you, so I'm going to give you two tickets for each night for you to give to whomever you wish." I gave Clint Eastwood tickets for one night and Goldie Hawn for the other night. And then Gary Busey arrived and he's sitting on the floor by the driveway and of course I'm called to remove him. But Gary was high, I'm not the kind of person to say that, that's not what I do, but everyone knew. I tried to tell him that he's not getting in and that he should get up off the dirt and out of people's

way and he agreed, saying, "Man you're right, I'm not meant to be here, but will you give him this gift from me." It was a photo of him with Eric Clapton, and of course I delivered it.

JIM BELUSHI: When Eric Clapton came and did those two shows in L.A. he only wanted real people going, no press, no industry people. He even had his own security guards so you couldn't sneak anybody in. I called his manager in London and got four tickets to each show. I brought my girlfriend and two friends one night, and I took another girlfriend and two friends the other night. One of those girlfriends ended up being my wife, and she's still pissed at me for it! We literally had the discussion three nights ago about it and she was shaking her head like, "You don't take me to a place and then the next night take a different girl to the same place." I go, "You're losing perspective, baby. I took you to see Eric Clapton. Nobody in town could get a ticket. I got the ticket. I took you to see Eric Clapton! You should be kissing my ass."

For bluesman Bobby Rush, it was the night that the Blues Foundation presented him with the B. B. King Blues Hero Award at House of Blues Cambridge.

BOBBY RUSH: I remember that I had tears in my eyes. I couldn't believe it! The only way for me to explain it to you was that I was speechless.

KEVIN MORROW: I remember the night Tom Petty got up there with Johnny Cash. I booked Johnny Cash four times, and still he was the only guy I ever really got nervous around, because he was my dad's idol. But Petty with Cash? That was pretty amazing. So many great nights come to mind, like the first time Kid Rock played with Lynyrd Skynyrd. That was amazing. Stevie Wonder was amazing. Elton John with Mary J. Blige was amazing. And one of the greatest performances of all time was Prince.

SONNY SCHNEIDAU: We put on a revue one time with Solomon Burke during Jazz Fest that lasted five and a half hours; it was like an encyclopedia

ABOVE: Elton John performing with Mary J. Blige at HOB L.A., February 2004. **OPPOSITE:** Bob Dylan performing at HOB Las Vegas.

ABOVE: Bootsy is never shy about bringing the funk to HOB.

of rhythm and blues—that's one of those nights that was really spine tingling.

JIM BELUSHI: I've seen them all. I remember seeing Tom Jones. I saw him do "Hard to Handle." I always thought Tom Jones was kind of that '60s, women-throwing-their-underwear-up kind of guy. But I saw his show and I was humbled. He was the greatest. I've seen Prince there also, as well as ZZ Top.

JONNY "2 BAGS" WICKERSHAM: Without a doubt, my most memorable night was the night Billy Gibbons sat in with us on a couple of songs.

MELISSA ETHERIDGE: Before I performed there I went in to watch the shows because they had great acts. I went to see Joan Armatrading; I remember seeing that Neil Diamond impersonator, Tom Sadge, and he was amazing. And I played there with Tenacious D once.

NORWOOD FISHER: The first time we played House of Blues was in Los Angeles. It was like entering a rock-and-roll Disneyland. Just being there on the Sunset Strip was an amazing occurrence. There was an excitement to being there, knowing the legend of the other House of Blues. The vibe was electric, the sound system was amazing, and the stage crew was top-notch and professional. The party atmosphere was just incredibly festive, nothing like what people sometimes expect from jaded L.A. audiences. The first time we played a House of Blues we ripped it, and the crowd loved it. We've had lots of amazing shows, but one of my favorites was with De La Soul, the Goodie Mob, and Joi. It was two incredible, sold-out nights at House of Blues Los Angeles. Both were out of this world and peak moments for us, and there was mutual love and respect for everybody on the stage. To have all that under one roof was incredible. We played at almost all of the clubs and had an amazing time at all of them.

THE SUNSET WATER TOWER

There's a water tower perched above the cotton gin–looking juke joint on Sunset Boulevard at Olive Drive in West Hollywood. And it has conjured somewhat of an urban legend. Arich Berghammer, a man who's seen it all since the venue opened its doors eighteen years ago, reluctantly spilled the beans. "You mean the five days these five celebrities and rock stars spent in the smoke house up above?" Yes, that water tower. Berghammer continues, "I literally had to go up there and ask if I could just bring down the bottles because they were piling up and clinking. I could tell you the names of the people who were up there, but some you just wouldn't be allowed to use."

Dan Aykroyd isn't nearly as hesitant to tell all. But first he offers a history lesson. "Well, the water tower was a feature from the industrial landscape of America," he informs in that earnest and scholarly tone that only Elwood Blues can deliver. "Isaac built it, and he hollowed it out and put two couches and a coffee table and a couple of ashtrays up there. We used to go there and sit and smoke and drink. . . . And Woody Harrelson and Keith Richards and I had a wonderful party there the opening week."

It was April 22, 1994, to be exact, and it was going to be a legendary night for many reasons, not the least of which was because new investors Aerosmith were headlining for the opening of the third House of Blues location. "Danny and I had a trapdoor with a ladder put in the eaves that led to a back, back room inside the water tower," recalls the mischievous brainchild and founder of House of Blues, Isaac Tigrett. "It was an attic, but we had it all done up: I put in Persian carpets and Persian sofas, antiques, lamps, and a little side table, so it was really cool. It's where we would all go and smoke pot. And on the night Aerosmith was opening the club, Dan came strolling in with Keith Richards and says, 'Let's go up there and smoke some pot.' Then Bruce Willis showed up, and he was so in awe of Dan and Keith that he just sat quietly in the corner like a little child. In the meantime, Dan and Keith were smoking this heavy weed, while Aerosmith was onstage playing. They had arranged for Keith to come, and he said, 'Ah fuck, they say they're the Rolling Stones of America, but fuck, I didn't want to see them anyway!'" But Aerosmith wanted their guru Keith Richards to check out their set. Isaac remembers a few notes being sent up to them to the effect of, "Where's Keith?" and "We understand that Keith's here." "And we were just up there smoking our brains out having a big time," laughs Tigrett.

Tigrett's trusted general manager, Michael Grozier, was also there that night. He was close enough to Tigrett and Dan to opt for the fly-on-the-wall experience if he chose, but he was too intimidated by the talent. Grozier remembers, "There was a moment when I poked my head up there, but it was like getting a glimpse of Olympus—I was like, 'I gotta go!'"

Word quickly spread after that infamous Hollywood night. More celebrities found out about the club within the club within the club. Aykroyd laments, "We partied there until the fire marshal heard that we were smoking up there in that wood tower—and they buttoned that up pretty quick. We've never been up there since, because we could have burned the whole strip down."

HOUSE OF BLUES®

TOOTS
AND THE MAYTALS
PLUS OUTLAW NATION

TUESDAY • AUGUST 12 • 9PM

For over three decades, Toots and the Maytals have charged Jamaican popular music with the fervor of American gospel-rooted soul and Toots' evangelistic stage delivery. Their unique combination of gospel, ska, soul and reggae molded their sound and made them rightful godfathers of ska and reggae music.

hob.com • 225 DECATUR • 504-310-4999 • ticketmaster

MARK PRINCI: Opening night in New Orleans we had a reggae star, Eek-A-Mouse, who came out with an enormous spliff. This was kind of dodgy, for us to allow someone to smoke out in the open like that. So Nigel said to him, "Sir, I don't mean to be impolite, but would you mind smoking that in the greenroom?" He turned around to Nigel and said . . .

NIGEL SHANLEY: "A rastaman don't smoke ganja in secret!"

MARK PRINCI: And then he put it out in Nigel's champagne and walked away.

CARLOS SANTANA: Oh, yeah, I saw Third World—Johnny Clegg's band from South Africa—and, man, I was rocking so hard. I was in the audience

and thought, "Wow, this is a good night to be in the audience!"

CHALI 2NA: Of course, I saw some great hip-hop shows. I saw Jay-Z on a couple of occasions, Eminem on a couple of occasions, and Wu Tang Clan, but let me tell you something, when I opened for James Brown with Ozomatli, that

ABOVE: The mighty Frederick "Toots" Hibbert of Toots and the Maytals performing at HOB Cambridge.

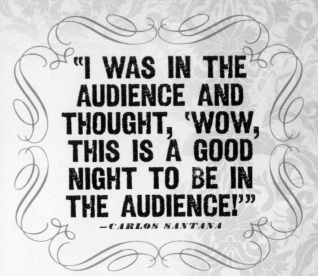

was crazy! First and foremost, I was starstruck. Brown was walking around the hallways and I was like, "That's James Brown! There's no other person in this industry that is as legendary as this guy here!" I remember how exciting it was to play, then get changed and run back out to the crowd so I could see him for myself.

KEVIN MORROW: I'll never forget this show. So James Brown pulls up early in what can only be described as a motorcade—his American-flag-adorned-limo, his buses, and four police motorcycles. Then James Brown rolled down the windows, looked around, and got out of the limo, almost like Patton or MacArthur walking Normandy Beach or something. He goes, "Where's Mr. Aykroyd?" I introduced myself and told him it was an honor to meet him but Danny wasn't there yet. He huffed and I showed him around, and then he walked over and bought like twelve pairs of boots at the boot store next door.

Bill Higgins of the Los Angeles Times was on the scene and provided the reportage on the Godfather of Soul's shopping spree in Monday's paper. "Observed: Early in the evening, Brown was piqued when a scheduled press conference was late. With his formidable entourage in tow, he stormed out of the club. He ended up buying boots at the nearby Paris Go store. The dialogue in the James Brown method for rapid footwear purchase is: 'You got 8D? You got blue? OK, gimme three pair of black. You got 8 in this? Eight in that? OK, that's enough.' Though Brown wanted to leave for dinner, he was persuaded to return to the club."

ISAAC TIGRETT: When I get back to the club I find out that the opening band, Taj Mahal, went on late.

KEVIN MORROW: Then you had John Lee Hooker, Isaac Hayes, Charlie Musselwhite, the Blues Brothers, and then James Brown. Halfway through the night, my production manager comes up to me and goes, "We're in big shit! James Brown is upset." I went over to him and said, "How are you doing, Mr. Brown?" and he goes, "What time do I go on?" I looked at him and told him around midnight. Then he asks, "and what time is it?" I looked at my watch and said "12:15," to which he replied, "I've lost all respect for you as a professional and a human being!"

ISAAC TIGRETT: As incredible as we were to the artists, and as beautiful as our greenrooms were, James Brown was always determined to stay in his bus, period. Now Dan's getting onstage with Jim Belushi, who was making his official debut as a Blues Brother, and I'm hoping that James Brown is OK. But he's not OK. We were running an hour late and somebody comes up to me and says, "James Brown wants to see you right now; he says he's leaving." I run out to the Super Bad bus that he's got, and he says to me, "I'm leaving right now! I'm supposed to be on right now and they've got them Blues Brothers up there! I'm telling you, I'm leaving right now!" I pleaded with him, "Mr. Brown, please, please, please!" and he answered, "You get them Blues Brothers off the stage or I'm leaving right now!" I rush backstage and make contact with Dan Aykroyd, who's only on the second song of their set. "James is gonna leave if you don't get off the stage right now! But

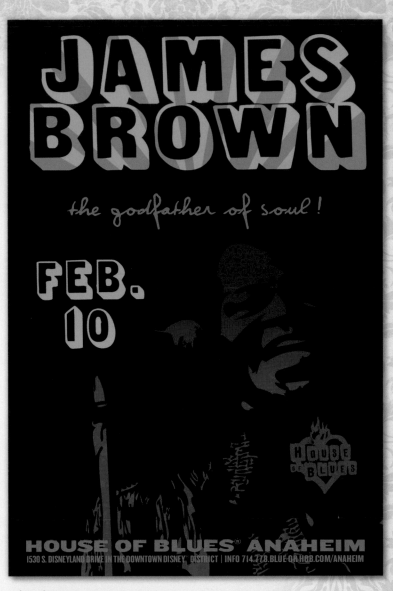

do whatever you want; it's your show." Then Dan went back to the microphone with, "Thank you very much! Mr. James Brown will be coming in just a few minutes!"

FRANKIE "KASH" WADDY: James was a funny character. He was so powerful and yet he had his own little thing, his backstage ego thing. He might look at playing a show like he's doing House of Blues a favor, 'cause that's how he is. But it's okay—Dan Aykroyd knew that. Whatever he asked for, he paid him more. He was letting him know, "Hey, you're James Brown and I'm not." You know? So he doesn't got nothing to prove. He'd already done it.

Like the Godfather of Soul, House of Blues has a track record that leaves them with little to prove. But as any dedicated entertainer knows, it's not their curriculum vitae that makes people feel good—it's dishing out the heat time and time again that makes people keep givin' it up and turnin' it loose.

OPPOSITE: James Brown performing at HOB L.A., November 16, 2005. **PAGES 110–111:** B.B. King performing with his band at HOB Anaheim, February 22, 2013.

chapter four

CROSSROADS OF DINING:
OR HOUSE OF BAM!

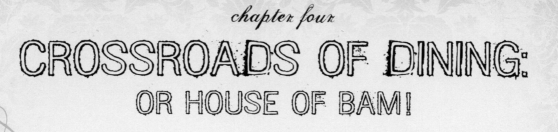

Artists who perform at House of Blues love coming back—not only for the fat-sounding stages, hot showers, and great greenrooms but also for the food, which isn't just good-for-a-venue good, it's real-deal good. More than a mere regional sampling of cuisine from Robert Johnson's Crossroads, the in-house eatery—called Crossroads at House of Blues—puts out a diversity of dishes reflective of its eclectic palate and its sincere dedication to Southern hospitality—which is some serious hospitality.

DAN AYKROYD: [The food is] completely Isaac; he's been eating southern Louisiana cuisine all his life. His nanny, Drewcilla, would prepare fried chicken, okra, and maple bread pudding, and he would also eat at all those great New Orleans restaurants, like Commander's Palace and Brennan's.

ISAAC TIGRETT: What else did I know about? I've never been trained or taught anything, so I got my mother's cook, Etta-B, to come over with her apple pie recipe. The bread recipe came from Simpson's grocery store down the street from me; the ice cream recipe came from the Klinke Brothers in Memphis. [These staples were] all from my roots in Southern culture and food.

Much of the menu may reflect Tigrett's childhood in the South, but many of the dishes are eatable postcards representing his travels, a portfolio of explorations in indigenous comfort foods everywhere. Because as exotic as a dish may sound to a diner, somewhere in the world that dish—whether it's clam chowder or tandoori chicken—is considered home cookin'. Beyond serving dishes, House of Blues serves culture, and the food is curated like the works of art on the walls and the talent on the stage.

MICHAEL GROZIER: Our original menu consisted of "international peasant food"—that's how Isaac summed it up. Bangkok Thai sticks and pad Thai noodles, Boston clam chowder, jambalaya, and tandoori chicken from India. I'll never forget Isaac coming back from a board meeting with the Harvard guys [the early investors]. They had asked him, "Why don't you just poll your customers and find out what they'd like to eat?" Isaac replied, "I am not going to have people tell me what they want to eat; I'm going to tell people what they ought to try—what they *should* eat." And that's when he came up with the pad Thai noodles and other dishes that were considered home cooking for regional indigenous people. Every dish means something. At House of Blues, it's always about the discovery, whether it's the discovery of the music or discovery of the art or discovery of the cuisine.

ABOVE LEFT: Buttermilk Fried Chicken, a Southern staple at Crossroads at House of Blues. **ABOVE RIGHT:** Early Crossroads at House of Blues flyer featuring HOB cofounders Isaac Tigrett and Dan Aykroyd. How about some lunch! **OPPOSITE:** B.B. Blues Bar, HOB Orlando.

The fare served at Crossroads is also much more than a prized collection of rec-ipes. It is the result of a collaboration with some of the most creative geniuses in the culinary arts. It's only logical that if the artists who rock the house are put up on a pedestal, then so too should the celebrity chefs who take up residency in its kitchens. And even after chefs like Aarón Sánchez end their residency, their signature meals remain part of the permanent collection. Unlikely as it seems, this concept was the brainchild of a man who wasn't originally associated with food at all: Shep Gordon. Gordon is probably most famous for managing the career of music legend Alice Cooper, but years before there was a medium like the Food Network, Gordon saw a future where cooks would become famous in their own right and hounded by groupies of the culinary persuasion.

SHEP GORDON: Around the time House of Blues opened, I started managing many of the world's great chefs: Emeril Lagasse, Nobuyuki "Nobu" Matsuhisa, Alice Waters, Paul Prudhomme, and the whole gang. Having come from the music business, where songs could be copyrighted, I wanted to see if I could develop a mentality of giving royalties for recipes. I sat down with

ABOVE: Crossroads pairs new American cuisine such as Lobster Mac & Cheese (left) with Delta favorites such as Shrimp and Grits (right).
TOP: Junior Wells working up an appetite during an early blues night at HOB Cambridge.

Isaac and said, "Listen, you've got this thing going, and I can bring you these big-time chefs to cook in your Foundation Room. I'll bring them in for a couple of days at a time, and if you agree to keep one or two of their dishes on your menu downstairs at every House of Blues, and pay them a royalty, then I think we can make something nice happen." And we did.

MICHAEL GROZIER: We were doing celebrity chef dinners in Foundation Room clubs. Ken Franks was our Foundation Room chef, and then I think we had Todd English. We worked with Shep Gordon back in the day; he was the first guy to really see the wave of chefs as artists, in a more commercially viable, outside-the-kitchen way.

ISAAC TIGRETT: We did the celebrity chef menu at the Los Angeles House of Blues in conjunction with the James Beard Foundation. I let Shep run the show because he was the man; he was a gourmet chef and an ultimate groupie of all the best chefs. Every month we'd bring in people like Emeril Lagasse and other leading chefs from New York and France, and every month we'd be booked beyond belief. The idea really

appealed to me because I knew that gourmet lovers in L.A. were so fickle that it would be hard to have a restaurant with only one chef. First it's the biggest thing, then they move on to the next chef, and the restaurant closes two years after that. But if we could have a new chef every month, patrons would come back. I said, "Fantastic! The chefs would come for three days and come out in their whites to meet the press and the supergourmets who were desperate to meet them, and their sous chefs would stay for another two weeks and teach us their menus. We'd get all their ingredients, all their gear, and slowly our team would be doing their stuff and adding dishes to our own menu." This was the beginning of the "celebrity chef," before they started opening up their own restaurants.

SHEP GORDON: We brought in a lot of guest chefs: Emeril Lagasse, Dean Fearing, Todd English, Sam Choy, and Larry Forgione. These were star-studded events—Alice Cooper was there, Sharon Stone, Michael Douglas, Rodney Dangerfield, Shari Belafonte, Arsenio Hall, Sammy Hagar, Emilio Estevez, and I remember a lot of basketball players, too.

ABOVE: Sammy Hagar (right) in the kitchen at HOB L.A. with celebrity chef Emeril Lagasse.

The dishing didn't stop in the restaurant, or upstairs in the exclusive Foundation Room. McIlhenny Co. (the makers of Tabasco) and House of Blues Foundation published the Cookin' Up the Blues cookbook. The book features recipes from blues masters–cum–gourmet chefs like Buddy Guy (and his Seafood Okra Gumbo), Clarence "Gatemouth" Brown (and his Religious Corn Muffins), and Tinsley Ellis (who shares a secret recipe for Grillades and True Grits). The book also includes colorful photos of works from House of Blues' Art Collection. Speaking about the book at its release in 1994, blues legend Koko Taylor explained to the Orlando Sentinel how the music, the art, and the food are all connected to the blues: "Food relates to blues because they're both good for your body and good for your soul."

When House of Blues first opened its doors, the Food Network wasn't something that people set their DVRs to, but today it's home to its own reality stars, celebrity chefs, and cooking shows. Aarón Sánchez is one of those celebrity chefs (as seen on that network's Heat Seekers and Chopped) and, as part of House of Blues' 20th Anniversary celebration, he was invited to update the menu. "It's sort of American classics through my eyes, reimagined and reinvented," Sánchez explained. "I wanted to create a menu that I thought would be a representation of what I would like to eat: signature burgers, flatbreads, sliders, fried chicken. House of Blues attracts such a wide demographic; you have families, you have businessmen that are on lunch, you have younger kids that want to catch a show but don't have a lot of money, so you have to have something that can appeal and be accessible to a large audience—and our menu does that."

TOP (CLOCKWISE FROM BOTTOM LEFT): Jambalaya, a Crossroads classic. Aarón Sánchez recently added a number of signature burgers to the menu, among them the Juicy Lucy burger, stuffed with cheese and topped with pickled jalapeños and chipotle. The Crossroads also crosses into the fine dining realm with well-plated dishes like the braised short ribs, and appeals to the veg crowd with hand-stretched flatbreads topped with grilled veggies.
ABOVE RIGHT: Resident celebrity chef Aarón Sánchez. OPPOSITE: Etta James performing at HOB L.A., July 1999.

MICHAEL GROZIER: We've put great food out for twenty years. When we first started it was all about international peasant food, and over time it morphed into more Southern-influenced cuisine, with barbecue becoming more of a signature at one point. But we're always looking to keep things fresh and interesting, and there is still a lot of opportunity to be creative with our cuisine while remaining true to our roots.

And for House of Blues, staying true means more than sticking to international home cooking and Southern dishes—though both continue to be a keynote of a menu that boasts street tacos, shrimp and grits, and lobster mac in a single breath—it also means taking care of the talent.

MELISSA ETHERIDGE: The food's *good*. What's great is that if you play there, they'll give you dinner. And it's soul food, it's down-home. . . . I mean, my folks come from Arkansas and northern Louisiana, and House of Blues has got that soul food, yet there are healthy choices too. I mean, I love, *love* the preshow dinners that I get when I play there!

KEN JORDAN: New Orleans is a small venue, but it has a big celebration every Sunday. I've also had one of the best Bloody Marys I've ever had in my life at that House of Blues; they put a little splash of Guinness in it to give it some fizz!

HOUSE
OF BLUES

GOSPEL BRUNCH: PASS THE PRAISE, PLEASE

That "big celebration every Sunday" is House of Blues' Gospel Brunch, a venue-wide homage to soul, salvation, and Southern food—three things celebrated at Gospel Brunch presented by Kirk Franklin. Now you may or may not be a believer, you may have come to the Gospel Brunch because you heard it was the most delicious buffet this side of heaven and the most fun you can possibly have praising the Lord (whomever that may be for you, as the Gospel Brunch is nondenominational). But you should know that, despite the show Franklin and the other performers put on, these people are the genuine article.

Everybody talks about how the bird is the word, but inside any House of Blues on any given Sunday the congregation of regulars, visitors, and musical-anointers at Gospel Brunch wouldn't know the "Surfin' Bird" from Adam. It's the Gospel Bird they know to be the word: the family feast of glistening golden fried

chicken and other heartwarming comfort foods that have become a post-church tradition in most African American households in the South. Even though House of Blues updates its Gospel Brunch menu all the time, it still honors the staples: cornbread muffins with maple butter, homemade biscuits, country gravy, fried chicken, and Creole chicken and shrimp jambalaya, which is a nod to House of Blues' New Orleans connection. While the carnivores come for the savory selection of meats (from smoked turkey to prime rib), everybody, and that's everybody, comes back for the absolutely sinful desserts—the fruit cobbler is berrylicious, but it's the white chocolate banana bread pudding that most would choose to cap off their last meal.

The visionary behind Gospel Brunch, Isaac Tigrett, had nostalgia for his childhood in the South, and he had the idea of combining the joyful and spiritual healing experience of a gospel service with the delicious form of family bonding that comes over a home-cooked, elaborate buffet. The call and

---

TOP: Kirk Franklin performing with the choir at House of Blues' Gospel Brunch.
OPPOSITE: Madeline Thompson fulfilling her role as Gospel Brunch mistress of ceremonies at HOB L.A.

response of an interactive musical performance happens in the same concert hall as the buffet, where, unlike in a conventional church, a burlesque act might have gone down in the same room the night before. Tigrett used to say, "Gospel Brunch cleaned from the atmosphere everything that went on those six days before."

To say that Tigrett was on to something with the Gospel Brunch would be an understatement. Rather than drawing a few stragglers looking for something to do with their Sunday, Gospel Brunch was "the one show that outsold every other show, no matter who was playing the whole week," Tigrett brags.

wheelchairs or yell "I can see!," but there is clearly more going on at Gospel Brunch than food and entertainment. People do exhibit a sense of healing and bliss as they sing "Amazing Grace." Most of the time it's totally unexpected, from people who never thought they had it in them to bawl and shout, people who thought they were coming for the smoked salmon, the homemade waffles, or the omelet station.

"We get so many testimonies from people. It's just a blessing," says Madeline Thompson of the legendary gospel group the Clara Ward Singers (who have appeared on the *Johnny Carson Show* and

He was impressed with the local Cambridge audience at the first House of Blues, where they tested the idea out. "I couldn't believe what I was seeing," Tigrett remembers. "Those Yankees were crying and carrying on, and standing on top of their chairs, just like when I was back in Jackson, Tennessee." And soon, the little House that never took reservations was booking them weeks in advance to accommodate the masses being turned away. Soon more shows had to be added, and Tigrett appointed Sylvia St. James to scout the most talented musicians from the local churches and teach them the program.

Back in House of Blues Los Angeles the Gospel Brunch is beginning to get as star-studded as Foundation Room clubs. Gospel Brunch is a "spiritual appetizer." Maybe people don't get out of

many others in their day) and a spirited mistress of ceremonies in Los Angeles. "I'm just blessed. Today Chris Bolton [the MC and lead vocalist] was singing the song 'Whatever You Need It's Already Done,' and I had to leave the stage because tears started to fall. I didn't want people to misunderstand, but that's how blessed I felt. What's really a blessing is when I see children clapping their hands and dancing to our music. There's nothing better than that."

Lead singer Chris Bolton doesn't take his role lightly; it's almost as if he's taken an oath to bring love and healing. "It's a wonderful experience to see the people come and be blessed with some great food and a gospel good time. To see all the generations come down here is a blessing, and to be able to minister to them in song is my gift." Bolton gets even

ABOVE: Chris Bolton gettin' down during a Gospel Brunch performance at HOB L.A.

more heartfelt. "It's uplifting and encouraging. You don't always know what people are going through, but a simple song can brighten somebody's day. So our mission is to encourage the people and let them know that it doesn't matter what's going on, because when they get to House of Blues, everything is going to be okay. It almost feels like medicine."

As part of its 20th Anniversary celebration, Gospel Brunch has been updated by the king of gospel, Kirk Franklin, who, in full-circle fashion, delivered one of the funkiest, most legendary Gospel Brunches ever back in that "pop-up" of a juke joint, House of Blues Atlanta, during the Atlanta Summer Olympics in 1996. Since then, Kirk Franklin has been a multi-platinum-selling purveyor of majestic fusions of gospel and contemporary music, and a mirror of Christian humanity boldly reflecting what one faith-walking man can accomplish. Franklin is a pioneer in gap-bridging musicianship, uniting audiences across gospel, hip-hop, pop, and R&B. His irresistible rhythms and rhapsodies have resulted in albums that consistently top both *Billboard's* Gospel and Christian charts, as well as ascend triumphantly into the Top 10 of the R&B/Hip-Hop chart. Franklin is also the host and executive producer of the gospel

talent show "Sunday Best," the highest-rated gospel program in BET network history, now heading into its sixth season. To date, the trendsetter has garnered nine Grammy Awards, thirty-nine Stellar Awards, sixteen Dove Awards (CCM), eight NAACP Image Awards, two BET Awards, an American Music Award, a Soul Train Award, and numerous others.

And yet, with all of his success and acclaim Franklin remains, at heart, a man who comes from shaky circumstances that could have paralyzed his spiritual growth within his humble familial beginnings. He is never far from that frightened and forlorn young man who didn't always know which way to turn. The heart of who Kirk Franklin is and his story struck a resounding chord with his fans years ago, and they have remained loyal ever since. He has never hidden behind his celebrity status but has remained connected to his audience through his music and candid discussions of life issues, which is what makes Franklin one of the most relatable and respected messengers in his field.

"House of Blues' Gospel Brunch is an American institution, so I am honored to be working hand in hand with them to revitalize the experience for music fans of all ages," beamed Franklin. Salvation has never sounded, or tasted, so good.

ABOVE: House of Blues has an uncanny knack for bringing variegated delights together under a single juke joint roof, and the Gospel Brunch—a perfect pairing of great food, singing, and salvation—is no exception.

chapter five
FOUNDATION ROOM

If "the road of excess leads to the palace of wisdom," the Foundation Room is where young sages get their ticket to ride. William Blake's passage from *The Marriage of Heaven and Hell* presaged a day when the hedonism and decadence that go down in the exclusive club—sometimes of Studio 54 proportions—would be harnessed and converted into a means of giving back to the community. A portion of all membership fees to Foundation Room clubs go into the piggy bank of the International House of Blues Foundation—a charity that partakes in community outreach and encourages youth to fully engage in music, art, and social awareness. The elegant speakeasy is a showcase of the community that can be built when diverse people (some with deeper pockets than others) who are passionate about philanthropy, music, and living la dolce vita come together under one posh roof. It's altruism that's much more than an afterthought—it's in the concept, it's in the name.

The Foundation Room is an exclusive yet approachable club within most House of Blues locations, many of which have different themed rooms alongside a main bar and lounge. These exquisite nooks can accommodate private dinners and offer secluded spaces where guests can have an intimate party before or after a show, while the bar and lounge area is perfect for a DJ set or an exclusive live performance. The Foundation Room in Los Angeles, for example, features the Prayer Room, which is split into the Buddha Room and the Ganesh Room, both of which are bathed in an amber glow and adorned with Indian tapestries and historic artifacts. The Captain's Room, with its floor-to-ceiling mahogany and mother-of-pearl inlay, feels as personal, organic,

and precious as a custom Gibson Les Paul. The City Lights room is just that, tempting patrons with open-air dining and panoramic views of the skyline. Guests can then slink out to the Parish, the ultimate in chill-out lounges, detailed with Persian carpets, antique Indian temple screens, handcrafted mahogany furniture, and the Andrew Wood–created "Blues Gods" ceiling, where white reliefs of various rock and blues masters and mistresses overlook the scene. The atmosphere is electric, the appointments exotic and luxurious, and visitors feel like a million dollars just walking into the place—but not in the stuffy way that makes relaxing feel off limits. Perhaps that's why members often say the Foundation Room is more than a place to be—it's a place to belong.

ABOVE: Gujarat fabrics line the entrance to Foundation Room L.A. **OPPOSITE:** Carvings of Buddha overlook the plush appointments and Persian carpets of the Buddha Room at HOB Las Vegas. **PAGES 124–125:** Mural art by Scott Guion on display at HOB L.A.

ISAAC TIGRETT: I did belong to a lot of fine clubs in England when I was younger, mainly because of my father and his friend and business partner, Sir James Goldsmith. Mark Birley invented the whole celebrity nightclub game with Annabel's, which is in the Mayfair district of London. It was *the* place in the 1960s. Birley was my hero. To be a member you needed three other members to recommend you—so as membership grew the club still maintained a certain type of personality and quality of people.

Foundation Room clubs aren't about class structure, but I didn't want a bunch of assholes up there, because at the end of the day it's about the work that we are doing for the Foundation, for the kids. We have board meetings and decide how best to help the children. The members are some of the heaviest cats around, and they are there because they believe in it! Some people aren't members, but they were brought in as guests and could be trusted to be good people.

DAN AYKROYD: What Isaac did brilliantly with Foundation Room clubs was to style them after the old English clubrooms of London, where rock stars would hang out. A lot of it has to do with the plushness, the comfort of the furniture, the warmth of the wood, the antiques, and the fact that there are no modern edges other than the diamond flake bar. The fabrics also give you the sense of a turn-of-the-century English clubroom, which were so popular at the time of the Rolling Stones, the Beatles, the Animals, and Cream— these were the places where they hung out in London. With the attentiveness of the service, you realize you're in a VIP environment the first time someone speaks to you. Last, there's the five-star dining, which backs everything up and makes the experience sumptuous every time.

ISAAC TIGRETT: I grew up in the amazing genteel world of the South, of ladies and gentlemen, a world filled with music and graciousness. Then

OPPOSITE: Lord Ganesha, known as the remover of obstacles, overlooks the appropriately named Ganesh Room in HOB L.A. As many a Foundation member will testify, Ganesha effectively removes inhibitions, too. ABOVE: In addition to exclusive parties, the Foundation Room offers a five-star dining experience. Pictured is one of the dining rooms at HOB Dallas.

MARK PRINCI: One of the great things about Foundation Room clubs is the decor. It is probably the first and only time that Mississippi Delta folk art made out of broken glass, bottle caps, blood, and finger paint has been coupled with South Indian architecture and eastern European furnishings and cohered somehow.

DAN AYKROYD: The stand-alone value of the Foundation Room as an architectural piece is in keeping with the dynamic quality of Isaac's design and creative sensibilities. Most of the furniture is from his collection. He went around the world buying furniture just like William Randolph Hearst did—warehouses full. So we have prayer rooms from Indian palaces, and we have Victorian mantelpieces and cabinets. Foundation Room clubs in Los Angeles, Las Vegas, Chicago, Boston—wherever we have them—are probably the most hospitable, warm, and architecturally attractive rooms in whatever city they happen to be. You could build a stand-alone Foundation Room on top of a skyscraper in any city.

ABOVE LEFT: Much of the woodwork in the L.A. Foundation Room is from a maharaja palace bought in South India and meticulously reassembled. **TOP:** In addition to being a remover of obstacles, Ganesha is the Lord of Beginnings. One of the pre-opening ceremonies at every House of Blues includes an invocation of Ganesha. **ABOVE RIGHT:** The Foundation Room's outdoor patio at HOB L.A. is ideal for taking in summer nights and offers views of the city's skyline.

I became a wild hippie. But the next thing I know, my father is in partnership with Arm & Hammer and Sir James Goldsmith and John Paul Getty, and I'm being exposed to all these ancient objects and beautiful things, which influenced me in the design of the Foundation Room. I was eighteen years old and experiencing whole new worlds of craftsmanship and style. So when it came time for the Foundation Room, I wanted it to be one of the most genuine and gracious places in the world.

MARK PRINCI: Isaac bought a maharaja's palace in South India that was falling apart. In order to get it out of India, he had to take the woodwork out and have it fumigated before customs would release it. We had to break it up into separate pieces, but the antiques commission wouldn't let us take it apart unless we hired an Indian antiques dealer to fly to L.A. with us and

supervise the dismantling and reassembling. We also hired this genius American kid named Matt Brown who was very good at figuring out puzzles. Together, the Indian antiques dealer and Matt Brown filled all the doorways and window frames with this woodwork of extraordinary beauty.

MELISSA ETHERIDGE: I remember the first time I was invited to the Foundation Room—it was beautiful. It's got stuff from India along with blues art—it's funny how it fits so well together. It's got these perfect little booths, so if you're shy and want to get away from people you can hang

out in a little booth back there. It's a wonderful place. Since my first visit I've held a lot of my pre-show stuff and some functions there.

MICHAEL GROZIER: What I think is really cool about the Foundation Room is that it brings together like-minded music fans who wouldn't normally interact. You have a stockbroker next to a guy who owns his own plumbing company next to a professional athlete who's standing next to some celebrity. Everybody's hanging out and digging the music and feeling like they're a little part of something different.

Places like the Soho House didn't exist before the Foundation Room. All the private clubs and high-end joints in Las Vegas weren't around before we put the Foundation Room on top of Mandalay Bay. If you look back, you can see that all these things, to some degree or another, are influenced by Isaac's imagination. Yes, there were private clubs, but taking them beyond being private or beyond being unattainable is something we did. People feel good that we're a conduit for our members to help fund school programs put on by the Blues Foundation.

ABOVE: Standing Buddha Sculpture, Foundation Room, L.A. **LEFT:** Bottle service is just one of the many perks for Foundation Room members. **TOP:** Warm, well lighted, and plush, the Foundation Room bar at HOB New Orleans is one of the more inviting taprooms in the city.

FROM HEADBANGING TO ELBOW RUBBING

There are other ways to get up to the Foundation Room, and no, we're not insinuating nefarious favors for a backstage pass, Steel Panther style. Sometimes gaining access is even more rewarding when it is random, especially when you come for the show and end up hanging out with the band.

ANJALI RAVAL: One of the great unique features of our venues is the Foundation Room. They are the ultimate VIP rooms. You are immediately transported to India or Morocco, surrounded by gorgeous Persian rugs and textiles, beautifully adorned walls covered in colorful Gujarat tapestry, enormous wooden temple doors and statues of deities, and comfortable sofas decorated by plush pillows. You almost forget you're at a nightclub with a band playing onstage in the other room. Foundation Room clubs were originally launched as an exclusive, membership-only, you-have-to-know-so-and-so-to-get-on-the-list privilege. They quickly became one of the most popular hangs for celebrities and local businessmen and women who just wanted to party in a really cool spot. Because the Foundation Room is usually located just a few feet away from the artists' dressing rooms, they started to become known as the unofficial "backstage" area of our venues, because inevitably you ended up having a drink or hanging out with bands after their show. Talk about perks!

ARICH BERGHAMMER: A bunch of us with different-colored wristbands would walk the music hall floor, and quite often we would pick a regular husband and wife. There'd be a couple that I saw pull up, and I just knew the guy was in the construction business or something, and I'd walk over to them and wrap their wrists. That's because we're into making memories, experiences that they would never in a million years get to have. I'd seat them next to Prince and watch their heads explode. I can't tell you how many times we did that. You bring a regular Joe into a room, and there's Joe Namath and Joe Montana at one table, Santana at the next table sitting next to Xzibit. I'd tell them, "Look, no

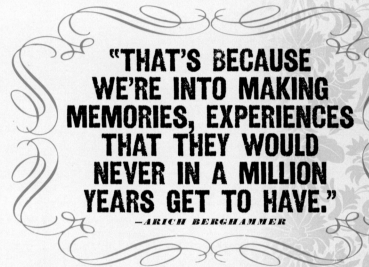

> ### "THAT'S BECAUSE WE'RE INTO MAKING MEMORIES, EXPERIENCES THAT THEY WOULD NEVER IN A MILLION YEARS GET TO HAVE."
> *—ARICH BERGHAMMER*

cameras, no recording, just chill and have a great time, and if your friends don't believe you, have them give me a call!"

ANJALI RAVAL: The Foundation Room allows people to rub elbows with artists and celebrities but maintains an exclusivity by being removed from the general public.

ISAAC TIGRETT: It's cool that fans can mingle with their favorite artists, but it's not cool to be there when someone walks in and goes, "Oh look, there's so and so! Let's get her autograph!" Anyone asking for an autograph is immediately thrown out, and our celebrities appreciate it. I don't care if the person is one of our main members or the head of a bank—no cameras and no autographs.

ABOVE: While cameras are not ordinarily allowed in Foundation Room clubs, occasionally they are. Here, one captures a glimpse of the sort of partying typical of the exclusive club.

MELISSA ETHERIDGE: It's true that it's nice when it's just a social thing and it's not, "Hey, can I have your autograph?" or "Can I take some pictures?" I've always been comfortable hanging out with whoever was in the Foundation Room. It's very well done and well thought-out.

MARK PRINCI: You can have a drink and shoot the shit with all kinds of people that you would never imagine you'd have access to, as long as it is just that—friendly people having a drink together. The minute the autograph books come out, it's over.

ARICH BERGHAMMER: Even our staff has to sign a nondisclosure and confidentiality agreement— every single one of them—because it's a place for celebrities to hang out besides someone's house in the hills; they come to the Foundation Room, where they won't be bothered. Isaac created this space where common folk like you and me could buy a membership, pay for the education of children, and sit down next to a rock star— because it's the music that is the driving force behind everyone being there. I can't tell you how many celebrities come to our venue, from Brad Pitt and George Clooney to Salma Hayek and Fran Drescher.

KEVIN MORROW: The ladies loved Tom Jones. There'd be everyone from Rosie Pérez to Fran Drescher going crazy over Tom Jones.

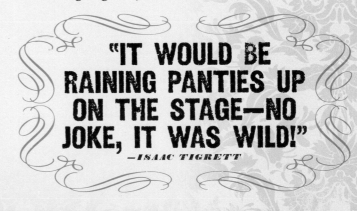

"IT WOULD BE RAINING PANTIES UP ON THE STAGE—NO JOKE, IT WAS WILD!"
—*ISAAC TIGRETT*

ABOVE: Carlos Santana frequents Foundation Room clubs not only for the party but also for the peace of mind that resonates in the Buddha Room.

MARK PRINCI: I've never seen women lose themselves like they did over Tom Jones. He would play, and women would throw their panties at him. And he'd be up in the Foundation Room hanging out and drinking and shooting the shit after the show—he was really cool. It helped that the artists' greenroom was on the same floor, right across the corridor, so there was a lot of traffic back and forth. They could have their privacy but also come out and share a drink with their fans.

ISAAC TIGRETT: Of course I remember Tom Jones in the Foundation Room. First, let me tell you, he would sell out in seconds! And all that talk about panties flying—I've seen it. It would be raining panties up on the stage—no joke, it was wild!

LONN FRIEND: One night there was an awesome MTV event after-party—this was at the peak of my visibility, when I was the editor of *RIP* magazine and on MTV as well as my own Saturday night syndicated radio show on Westwood One Network—I was standing by the wall next to Robert De Niro. This fan walked up to both of us and said, "Lonn 'fuckin' *RIP* magazine' Friend!" I swear! I said, "Hey, dude." I looked at De Niro, and he just smiled. He had really long hair like he did in *Cape Fear* or *Angel Heart* and was probably happy not to be recognized, but I had such reverence for him that this shout-out from this fan made me feel really awkward.

ARICH BERGHAMMER: I can't tell you how long I sat with Busta Rhymes when he was up in the Foundation Room, and O.D.B., too. First he said to me, "Dude, I'm going to blow you up." And I asked back, "Why would you want to do that?" Then we had a conversation over a couple of drinks.

CHALI 2NA: The Foundation Room has that velvet, exclusive feel. They've also got these little up-in-the-cut rooms that are bigger than they appear to be. I love that place. It's perfect for an after-party, and there is the chance that you will get to hang out with the people you came to see. In Los Angeles I've been up there with everybody from Busta Rhymes to Harrison Ford—all kinds of people come out. The place is exquisite enough

so the stars don't feel bad about coming to a small little club. They like the intimacy.

MARK PRINCI: I loved watching Dan Aykroyd interact with everyone in the Foundation Room. He'd act like you were Dan Aykroyd and he was a fan of yours interested in what you were doing. He was one person who didn't mind signing autographs and taking photos with fans.

DAVE KING: I love to hang out with people, and the Foundation Room makes it easy and pleasurable because all the rooms are beautiful. They've got beautiful bars, and you can chill out with friends and still like feel you're at the venue. And if I forget something in the dressing room, I just go down the hall and back to the dressing room. It's not like you're in a bar in another venue—you're still at the venue. It's great!

PAUL McGUIGAN: I was lucky enough to do a show with James Brown, and later on all the VIPs were up in the Foundation Room. It was amazing to see Dan Aykroyd and Bill Murray dancing around, hanging out, and having a good time with a bunch of random people. You can see Dan's connection to the club even to this day, because on any given night he's there buying everybody drinks. He's not just putting them on the tab and comping them out later; he's taking out his credit card and buying drinks on his own dime. "Drinks for everybody! And I'm paying."

SHEMEKIA COPELAND: I'm not much of a partier, but I definitely had a couple glasses of wine in the Foundation Room in New Orleans. That's a great House of Blues. I played there with Keb' Mo'.

Maybe it's because he worked there for almost twenty years, but Sonny Schneidau is also partial to his Foundation Room in New Orleans.

SONNY SCHNEIDAU: When I go to the Prayer Room, I sit at the feet of a two-thousand-year-old Buddha. This Foundation Room is just so lush and wonderful—the woodwork and the carvings and everything about the detail of this room are very, very special.

OPPOSITE: The Buddha evokes a sense of compassion, which is the heart of the concept behind the Foundation Room.

STUDIO 54 ON THE SUNSET STRIP

Forget 77 Sunset Strip. On many nights, the Foundation Room was more like Studio 54. Bianca Jagger wouldn't have been able to get in the elevator with a white horse, but some epic, extravagant, wild and crazy nights have taken place within those Persian-carpeted walls. Nights when the bold and the beautiful let their guard and their hair down, and party alongside fans, often to bacchanal proportions.

ABOVE LEFT: A four-armed Vishnu relief of South Indian origin.

ISAAC TIGRETT: There was a Studio 54 aspect to it. You'd walk in and there was Bob Dylan on the right and Jack Nicholson on the left.

JIM BELUSHI: Oh, I really can't comment on that [celebrity / Studio 54 party comparison]. I look at everybody the way I define myself—I'm a magic chaser. And performing onstage at House of Blues is magic for me. Being with Danny and playing is magic. Acting, between action and cut, is magic. And people want to go where there's magic. Whether you're Magic Johnson or Tom Johnson, you look for the magic, and House of Blues is magic.

Studio 54 had Steve Rubell, the stirrer of a glamorous and decadent cocktail. The Foundation Room had Nigel Shanley. Nigel never had an official title at House of Blues, which made him even more invaluable because it was those things he did that couldn't be documented or calculated—the intangibles of hosting—that made those deeds priceless . . . and almost mythical.

ISAAC TIGRETT: Nigel was my man inside the Foundation Room. He made sure all the members and their guests were properly cared for. He took care of them like no one else could. I designed the Foundation Room and put my character into it, but he lived the Foundation Room.

ARICH BERGHAMMER: If you took a snapshot of Isaac in the Foundation Room in those days, you'd see Mark Princi to Isaac's left and Nigel to his right. If you had to give Nigel a position it would be ambassador, but I would call Nigel our "vibe-rator." He made sure we had all the beautiful and connected people. When Hugh Hefner, James Caan, and Michael Douglas came in, it would be because of Nigel. When Sally Lear of the Learjet family came in, it was because of Nigel. And he'd be right in the middle of it.

MARK PRINCI: Nigel got around. He was a testament to knowing that the best private plane to be on was somebody else's.

ARICH BERGHAMMER: Nigel was magical, and he was there keeping the electricity alive. He was very close to Tom Jones, so he would be there until 5, 6, 7 a.m. I'd leave at 2 a.m. and come back at 8 a.m. for business, and he would just be leaving.

MARK PRINCI: We were fully committed to the idea that Isaac had, and he inspired us. One of the key ingredients was that we had no lives. I left my wife in France and lived in Isaac's house, and Nigel was unattached. We did nothing but eat and sleep House of Blues, night and day.

NIGEL SHANLEY: My personality is in the walls of the Foundation Room. It was my home, my haunt, and my life. I was always there and never took time off. After my first six months at House of Blues in L.A., Isaac sat me down and said, "I'm very upset with you! I heard you haven't had a day off yet." I asked, "Haven't I?" I didn't even realize it, but I loved what we were doing.

A legend about the day Nigel Shanley met Isaac Tigrett offers a lot of insight into the level of hospitality and pampering VIPs and their guests have come to expect. As the story goes, Isaac walked into the fancy restaurant in Sweden where Nigel was the manager and asked for a burger and a bottle of Dom Perignon. The restaurant didn't have Dom, so Nigel had the waiters distract Tigrett with a salad and some ice water while he ran to the restaurant's other location and got a bottle. When Tigrett ordered another bottle, Nigel repeated the charade. Only this time he was busted, and Tigrett called him over.

NIGEL SHANLEY: Isaac said, "I have a few questions for you. I'm not trying to embarrass you, but number one: Why did you go out and get that bottle of Dom? And number two: Why you, the manager, and not a busboy or someone else?"

I told him, "Well, no one would miss me if I was gone for ten or fifteen minutes, but if I send a busboy you're going to have a dirty table. If I send a waiter, someone will have cold food. And if I send the dishwasher, I won't have clean dishes to serve your food." I explained to Isaac that the dishwasher was the most important person in the business, and that without him you can't serve food and drinks, and then you have no business at all. That's when he smiled, pushed his card across the table, and said, "I'm going to change your life forever."

MARK PRINCI: Nigel was a generous and magnificent host. Dennis Hopper, Tony Curtis, Jack Nicholson, Clint Eastwood, gangster rappers, politicians—you name it, they all came into the Foundation Room and hung out with Nigel. You have no idea how hard it was to get into the Foundation Room in those early days. The place was always a scene, but if you knew the magic words "I know Nigel," then you had a chance. If I die and go to heaven, that's the first thing I'm going to tell St. Peter: "I know Nigel."

Nigel didn't have an official title, but he did have a directive—make the VIPs happy, at any cost. The Foundation Room became the hottest place in town, not just because of its Studio 54–like atmosphere but because the patrons were being catered to hand and foot, even if it meant going across the street for a bottle of Dom.

NIGEL SHANLEY: I found it amazing that I could get paid to be good to people. All I wanted to do was concentrate on people. I couldn't care less about the cost of serving a Heineken. I couldn't even spell the word *cost*. That was because I was a product of Isaac. He felt that if we weren't giving enough away, we weren't being good enough to our members. And believe me, I gave away the most.

ARICH BERGHAMMER: People thought Nigel owned House of Blues. He'd come to work when he wanted, and he'd hang out by the bar drinking Cristal with the guests. Sure, my management team would get pissed and ask me

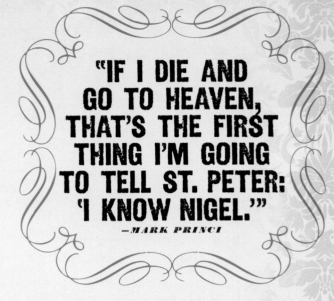

"IF I DIE AND GO TO HEAVEN, THAT'S THE FIRST THING I'M GOING TO TELL ST. PETER: 'I KNOW NIGEL.'"
—*MARK PRINCI*

why he was allowed to do it. I'd just say, "That's what he does. It's his job to schmooze, and it's not yours." I'd have a team meeting and sit Nigel in the corner. Then I'd remind them that they were all receiving bonus checks because every Playboy playmate was in the room because of Nigel, every rock star was here because of him, and he held their hands and knew their names and took care of their each and every "ism." "So be grateful."

NIGEL SHANLEY: Certain people, like Michael Grozier and Arich Berghammer, saw my value to the business. "Leave him alone; he's not going to embarrass us," they'd say. "In fact, he's going to make us look good." I became a verb. I remember I was in a small village in India visiting Sai Baba and someone called with a problem. Isaac said into the phone, "Lord, it's easy, just 'Nigel-ize' him." It was obviously a sweet compliment, but that's what I did.

ARICH BERGHAMMER: Nigel is right—it's another part of what Isaac stood for, what I call *conceptual integrity*. For example, Rick James came in all the time. One night, he and Teena Marie got up and walked out on an enormous check. Do you think I'm going to stop him? That's Rick James the Foundation members were partying with, and that's what they're going to talk about to all their friends whenever they talk about that night in the Foundation Room. So you better believe we're going to comp that check.

HOUSE OF SUPERFREAKS

Make no mistake, the Foundation Room is a classy place, but that doesn't mean things don't get nasty. It doesn't matter how breathtaking a room is—if it's got no funk, if it's got no stank, then it's got no mojo. And sometimes that means things get a bit naughty.

ARICH BERGHAMMER:

One of my fondest memories was when we did the first ViViD Christmas party. I will never forget it as long as I live. It was a private event in the Foundation Room, and I got a phone call from one of my managers saying, "Dude, you've got to come here and see what's going on in the Ganesh Room!" I peeked my head in and there were like twenty people starting to really get down. I would say to my team every night that we want our guests to go home and say, "You're never going to believe what I saw at House of Blues . . ." And if we give them a dot-dot-dot every night, we did our job—we win.

CHALI 2NA: I've seen some wild shit in the Foundation Room. I'll put it that way. I've seen everything from hella booty parties—big bubble booty girls dancing around half naked—to chaps, how do I say this as PG as possible, getting . . . you know . . .

Funny business aside, the Foundation Room was and is a great place to dine, toast your friends, and catch a private performance—from go-go dances and heavy metal book readings, to space-age DJ sets and resident bands, to once-in-a-lifetime performances by iconic and even knighted legends.

LONN FRIEND: My friend Scott Ian from Anthrax was doing that *VH-1 Supergroup* show with Evan Seinfeld, Jason Bonham, and Sebastian Bach, and I was about to launch my book, *Life on Planet Rock*, and wanted to read some chapters somewhere. So Scott goes, "Let's do it at House of Blues!" We did it in the Parish Room, right behind the Foundation Room, which is a really cool, vibey room. Every week I came in and read a different chapter. Scott was friends with Patton Oswalt, who came down to read my Kiss chapter. We had several hundred people in there. They brought down a screen and we watched *Supergroup* live on VH-1. The room was jumping and everybody had an awesome time.

NIGEL SHANLEY: We had a piano in the Foundation Room in those days, and I

remember Elton John coming in and just tinkling. It was a beautiful night.

Some of the hottest DJs and electronic acts, from Steve Aoki to Deadmau5 and the Crystal Method, have played the Foundation Room, and Paul McGuigan made sure the sound was up to snuff for the club culture.

PAUL McGUIGAN: When I came in, we reinforced the sound of the Foundation Room in order to meet the demands of the music being played, because even though EDM wasn't big yet, DJ culture was always part of the Foundation Room. I love seeing the mix of people in the room. You have people there to see a rock-and-roll show, Foundation members in their fifties, and the EDM kids invited by the DJs—and they're all on the dance floor having a great time. The place is special because you've got these electronic music heads rubbing elbows with Jay-Z and Beyoncé and Rihanna, along with the artists they came to see that night. It's the embodiment of that whole "unity through diversity" thing that House of Blues has. It makes the Foundation Room such a special place.

ABOVE: As Aykroyd explains, the HOB Foundation Rooms are "probably the most hospitable, warm, and architecturally attractive rooms in whatever city they happen to be." And Foundation Room Las Vegas is no exception. **OPPOSITE:** The intimacy of the Foundation Room makes it an ideal space for DJs to play underground cuts in front of a hot, close crowd.

> ## "WE DIDN'T PROMOTE IT, WE DIDN'T ANNOUNCE IT, WE JUST STUCK HIS EMBLEM ON OUR ROOFTOP, LIKE THE BAT-SIGNAL."
> —*ANJALI RAVAL*

Then there was the night the Purple One made House of Blues his home away from home. Prince played every room in the house, literally.

ANJALI RAVAL: Prince is the epitome of House of Blues because of his vast musical background. The guy can get on the guitar and play his hits, he can rock out, he can play the blues—he can play it all. He got very comfortable here, and one day he called up, last minute, and said, "I want to come to the Parish." From midnight until four in the morning he held a concert there. He invited guests like Justin Timberlake and Cameron Diaz, and all those folks walked into the Parish and mingled

ABOVE: Prince is perhaps the only artist iconic enough to simply shine his symbol on a venue's facade and draw a crowd, and House of Blues L.A. is perhaps the only venue gutsy enough to do it.

and ate from a spread of his favorite vegan food prepared by our chef. There was a short stint when Prince would host his intimate jam sessions in our Foundation Room for his invited guests. Sometimes they jammed; sometimes they just hung out and listened to music. And then there were times when he would agree to perform shows for his fans. In May 2011, he performed three sets in three different rooms within the venue. He started the night on the main stage and performed a very cool eclectic set for about eight hundred fans. He then did the second set on our restaurant stage for about two hundred fans. He ended the night, solo, just shredding on his guitar for about one hundred people in the Foundation Room lounge. We didn't promote it, we didn't announce it, we just stuck his emblem on our rooftop, like the Bat-Signal. He brought out all the stars for that night, including Tom Cruise, Bono, Larry Mullin Jr., and our friends from No Doubt. Again, just a great example of how a music fan is really just a music fan in the end.

Star-studded, decadent, and just the right amount of lecherous, Foundation Room clubs bring swank to the House of Blues juke joint. It's the house of the private party, but the community outreach it was designed to fund is anything but exclusory.

ABOVE: Prince performing on the main stage at HOB L.A. in June 2004.

chapter six

VISUAL BLUES

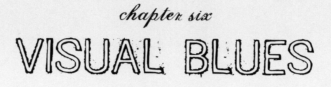

On Saturday, November 23, 1996, two nights before the opening of House of Blues Chicago, Gregory Warmack—a Chicago artist better known as Mr. Imagination—was asked to lend a little artistic flair to the location for its grand opening. He worked tirelessly during the next forty-eight hours, embellishing the barroom with colorful bottle caps of the sort that adorned his customized twenty-pound top hat. And he went on to do pieces for House of Blues in Orlando, Las Vegas, and Houston. Mr. Imagination wasn't the only artist to do bespoke installations for House of Blues, nor the only one whose style and approach was close to its juke joint aesthetic and philosophy. Like many of the self-taught artists represented by House of Blues, Warmack's work is bricolage, each piece a pastiche of found objects—colorful, vibrant, and soulful—not unlike the "Crazy Quilt" that graces every stage. It is beautiful, yes, but as early folk art collectors Chuck and Jan Rosenak describe in their guide, *Contemporary American Folk Art*, it is also "about the black experience and Warmack's search for his African roots," and it tells a story that makes it a sort of blues for the eyes. For a time Warmack lived in an abandoned house over which he hung a sign, also made of bottle caps, that read, "Welcome to the World of Mr. Imagination." While that sign never made it to House of Blues, the salutation—perhaps without the prefix—could certainly hold its own alongside the ubiquitous *ALL IS ONE*. Indeed, if House of Blues' Art Collection could utter a collective mantra, it would likely be "Welcome to the World of Imagination."

But it took more than imagination to begin what would become the most extensive folk art collection on permanent display; it also took foresight, good taste, and dedication to cultivating a thoroughgoing bluesy vibe, not to mention a fair dose of guru-given luck. Isaac Tigrett often sought advice from Sathya Sai Baba, but several people believe that Sai Baba was capable of lending a helping hand even from afar. Just ask Michael Feder, the man responsible for procuring and cataloging most of the folk and outsider art premiered at the Cambridge House of Blues and other venues.

MICHAEL FEDER: The juke in my own case was in the art of people like "Mose T." Tolliver, Jimmy Lee Sudduth, Leroy Almon Sr., and many others. I had a compulsion to collect it because I felt it was the visual representation of the blues. People told me I was deranged, but I moved to Los Angeles and, together with some partners, got a warehouse where I started to catalog the stuff. It was primitive—basically a photo album—but for me it was specific: African American art from 1960

OPPOSITE: Mosaic of Clarence "Gatemouth" Brown, on display at HOB L.A. This tribute to Gatemouth was created by the students of the Alliance Community Day School under the guidance of artist Ramesees with the support of IHOBF and The Village.

to 1990 from the Deep South. When Isaac was working on the Cambridge House, he was going around from gallery to gallery but couldn't find what he was looking for. He panicked on the phone to Sai Baba, saying, "My club is opening in two weeks, and I still haven't found it." Sai Baba responded by telling him not to worry, that he would send him the solution, and hung up. Thirty seconds later I rang Isaac's doorbell with my portfolio in hand. Since then I've had this permanent philosophy: "You never know when your guru's gonna call."

ISAAC TIGRETT: I can remember the knock at my door at eight in the morning. Michael Feder was standing there saying, "I hear you're into all this art and you're opening a place in Cambridge." I said yes, and he pulled out his catalog with over two hundred pieces that he said no one wanted to buy. I flipped through the book and said, "I'll take it all!" That's when Boston started to come together.

MICHAEL FEDER: At Isaac's place we looked through the original portfolio that became the look of House of Blues. He said, "Michael, this is House of Blues and I need it right away. How soon can you send it up there?" And he wrote me a check on the spot.

MICHAEL GROZIER: Let me tell you—watching Isaac create Cambridge House was like sitting there with Michelangelo while he's painting his masterpiece. It was clearly his vision.

ABOVE: Part of the creative genius behind House of Blues' Art Collection is the pairing of American folk art (right) with art inspired by Eastern religious traditions, such as the Hamsa hands (left) on display.

The masterpiece that was Cambridge House inspired the look and feel of every House of Blues, each a juke joint–cum–music hall–cum–barroom–cum–art gallery that, together, housed (but housed is not the right word, more like thrived alongside) a diverse and storied collection of art. Indeed, if folk art is the visible blues—full of raw emotion and hard knocks—House of Blues is its home.

By the tally of House of Blues' current curator, Scott Smith, there are more than ten thousand works in House of Blues' Art Collection, which makes it one of the largest repositories of American folk art in the world. A portion of the collection has spent time on the road as well: In the summer of 2013, the Ogden Museum of Southern Art curated an exhibition entitled When You're Lost, Everything's a Sign: Self-Taught Art from the House of Blues, which highlighted roughly two hundred pieces. But it's amid the lively atmosphere of House of Blues that the works really show their character. "We consider ourselves a living museum. There's nowhere else in the

world where you can experience the whole [blues] culture: taste the food, hear the music, see the visual expression," explained former house curator Carole Crittenden to the Florida Times-Union in 1998.

DAN AYKROYD: Where else can you see a show from the bar or from your seat and also look at a wall of art that celebrates rural Southern culture and African American culture?

TOP: *Crazy Fish by* American folk artist Glenn Fox. **ABOVE RIGHT:** The stages themselves are unique works of art, blending spirituality and American folk with the religious symbols of nearly every faith framing the stage and the African American-style "Crazy Quilt" that is a keynote of every venue.

The art pieces on the walls are as diverse as the artists who perform on the stage, but there is still a clear aesthetic at work. That aesthetic was once identified as outsider art, a literal designation meaning the artists and their works resided outside the fine art canon. Today the collection is characterized by a much more dignified, if not more pretentious, term: Southern vernacular art. The subject matter and the materials reveal the artists' state of heart and mind, as well as the environment in which the art was made. In creating these rural folk art masterpieces, the artists utilized whatever was available. Pieces of corrugated tin and planks of wood often substitute for canvas, and pigments made from wild berries stand in for oil and acrylic paints. Artists like Jimmy Lee Sudduth, Leroy Almon, Howard Finster, and "Mose T." Tolliver and his daughter, Annie Tolliver, among many others, expressed their realities through their art and drew inspiration from the same sources as bluesmen like B. B. King, Magic Sam, Lead Belly, Howlin' Wolf, and John Lee Hooker.

For Michael Feder, outsider art was nothing less than the visual juke joint. Dan Aykroyd and Isaac Tigrett express a similar opinion in an Access Hollywood episode dedicated to House of Blues, which aired on July 12, 1997. Aykroyd, playing the role of the interviewer, asks Tigrett how he came to the opinion that folk art is the perfect complement to House of Blues' "whole voodoo blues kind of thing." Tigrett answers, "Well, it's the visual blues. It comes from the same part of the country as [the blues]: Louisiana, Mississippi, Alabama, Kentucky, Tennessee. These are untrained artists, people who just had the gene inside them that said 'create.' They pick up whatever they can, whether it be Coke bottles, a piece of lumber, or tin, and now these artists have become some of the great heroes of folk art." Moments later, Tigrett explains, "God put that gene in them and said, 'Hey! Manifest yourself!'"

Artist Charles Gillam is known for his wood carvings of famous blues players, and blues hero Charlie "King of the Delta Blues" Patton was his first subject. He has carved vestiges of Robert Johnson (his totem poles always have Johnson at the top), Muddy Waters, and many others, including the beloved wood carving of Clarence "Gatemouth" Brown that can be seen next to Gatemouth's personal booth in the New Orleans House of Blues.

ABOVE: *Mermaid* by Calvin Livingston, on display at HOB L.A.

CHARLES GILLAM: I love the blues, I love the instruments, I love the research I have to do on the artist. It's like an energy thing—a spiritual thing that hits me and makes me carve these pieces out. It's hard to explain, but it's like the energy of the artist takes over me. You know, I watched some of the best self-taught artists, like Mr. Imagination and Herbert Singleton, and I wanted to be like them.

MICHAEL GROZIER: The importance of House of Blues' Art Collection is that it puts a new light on the creative process. The fact that you can still be creative without training or conventional materials shows that creativity has no boundaries. That you can make art by taking something and repurposing it into something else shows that we're only limited by our own experiences and our own imaginations.

TOP RIGHT: *Big Director* by Ruth Mae McCrane, on display at HOB L.A. **ABOVE:** *Blind* by Calvin Livingston, on display at HOB L.A.

LEROY ALMON SR.: *DEVIL FISHING*

This Georgian's signature wood carving expresses his religious and moral themes through a depiction of Satan hovering above God's green Earth and dangling a long fishing line rigged with multiple hooks and baited with vices. Explains Dan Aykroyd, "On one line there's a deck of cards, on one line there's a woman, and on another there's a whiskey bottle," all tempting the thrill seekers down below with carnal delights almost too enticing to resist.

ASSASSINATION

If Leroy Almon's depictions of the conflict linking human nature, religion, and morality look like they're right from the old blues lyrics of "Blind" Willie Johnson, then *Assassination* shows the artist moving on to the sociopolitical consciousness of late '60s / early '70s soul music. The piece represents the infamous assassinations of Abraham Lincoln, Malcolm X, Martin Luther King Jr., and John F. Kennedy, as well as a mysterious and racially charged crucifixion (the viewer is left to decide of whom). In *Devil Fishing*, Almon examines man's existential battle with a devil that taunts using earthly temptations, but *Assassination* explores his other central theme, which he described to folk art collectors Chuck and Jan Rosenak as "the African American experience—racism and how it affects black Americans."

Charles Gillam grew up in the Lower Ninth Ward, where his father would play guitar for the church on Sundays and in a blues band with future R&B legend Fats Domino on Saturday nights. He now curates his own outsider art museum, the Algiers Folk Art Zone and Blues Museum. For Gillam, the connection between his art and the blues is not only spiritual; it's also physical and material.

CHARLES GILLAM: When I'm carving blues icons like Muddy Waters, it's an honor. The spirits of those people come to me and show me how to carve it. I get my wood right from the Mississippi River near my house, and I look at it—it was waterlogged, then it drifted to the shores of the bank, and dried out and petrified—and think to myself, "Who knows, this could be one of the trees that one of these famous blues players used to sit up under and play their music." And the more I thought about those characters, the more the illustration would come forward. I feel their energy, and it reminds me of how my daddy used to sound on his guitar. When I do my art I listen to the blues and think about what was going through these guys' minds. I love the tone, and I sit down and interpret the words they're saying. I had to learn how to feel what these guys were feeling and put that feeling into my wood carvings—because I'm not only carving a piece of wood to make a dollar from it, I'm carving because it's an honor to pay tribute to the legacy of those artists.

In the same way that many visual artists sought to honor blues legends through their works, Tigrett sought to honor those visual artists not only by displaying their work but also by educating his staff about its significance. Michael Grozier recalls a field trip with Isaac Tigrett in early 1993, shortly after the opening of the Cambridge House of Blues and in anticipation of two new locations in New Orleans and Los Angeles.

MICHAEL GROZIER: We went to the ballroom of the Charles Hotel [in Cambridge], where all this outsider art—pieces that ended up going into four or five House of Blues venues—was laid out.

MICHAEL FEDER: I organized that shipment and sent the art up to Isaac at the hotel.

MICHAEL GROZIER: He bought so much stuff from artists like Leroy Almon, Jimmy Lee Sudduth, and Archie Byron. Isaac said, "Kid, what do you think about all this stuff?" I told him that I didn't get it and that it looked primitive and sophomoric. He said, "Kid, that's the beauty of it. These are people who created this art for the sheer purpose of creating. You see that one over there? Archie Byron? He works in sawdust and glue to create statues. And that guy, Jimmy Lee Sudduth, works with mud and root dyes and creates self-portraits, over and over. And see that guy over there? That's Howard Finster; one day God talked to him from his thumb and said, 'You should be painting!' He ended up doing album covers for the Talking Heads and R.E.M." After he explained the art, it mattered to me. We taught the staff about the different artists—who they were and why they did their art—and then the art mattered to them.

MICHAEL FEDER: As soon as I saw R. A. Miller's work in 1989, I was hooked. I bought every piece I could get. Then I discovered other artists and began collecting more of this kind of art. People came in and told me that it was junk, that it looks like a kid did it, and they even asked if I was the artist. Even my grandmother, may she rest in peace, said, "You're lucky you're not married because no woman could put up with all this crap!" I didn't think outsider art was a correct name because that could include art by Charles Manson—visionary art or Southern vernacular art is much more appropriate.

ABOVE: *Lord Love You* by R. A. Miller, on display at HOB L.A. **OPPOSITE:** *Glory Jesus Help Change* by Calvin Livingston, on display at HOB L.A.

GREGORY WARMACK (MR. IMAGINATION): *UNITY ARCH*

While recovering from a gunshot wound and subsequent coma, Gregory Warmack received visions of traveling through history and being both physically and spiritually connected with ancient civilizations. The experience inspired his moniker, Mr. Imagination, as well as renewed his effort to create ornate furniture and art objects. One of the most exhibited and critically acclaimed outsider artists, Warmack was commissioned to create *Unity Arch*, which visitors have to pass through in order to enter the Voodoo Garden at House of Blues Orlando. The installation is a mixed-media sculpture composed of cement over chicken wire and bejeweled with bottle caps (which Warmack called "magic material"), sticks, clothing, pieces of hardware, shards of glass, buttons, beads, and other found objects.

SELF PORTRAIT

Mr. Imagination's handiwork is all around House of Blues Chicago—as unique moldings and trimmings on and around the walls and in a series of self-portraits. Here is a detail from *Self Portrait*, a piece that combines an actual photograph of Gregory Warmack with interpretations of himself—in this case an old paintbrush transformed into a red face with bristles as his hair and a crown of buttons.

Of course, House of Blues was not the first place to house outsider or folk art. Mr. Imagination had a solo exhibit in 1983 at the Hammer Gallery in Chicago, and by the time that Tigrett opened Cambridge House in 1992, Mr. Imagination had been given a retrospective at the University of Illinois at Chicago. Mose Tolliver was included in an exhibit of black folk art at the Corcoran Gallery in Washington, DC, in 1982, and later he had a solo show at the Montgomery Museum of Fine Arts. The Phyllis Kind Gallery was exhibiting outsider art, first in Chicago, then in New York in the late '70s and into the '80s. And both Herbert Singleton and Charles Gillam were introduced to House of Blues through Barrister's Gallery in New Orleans. Still, House of Blues has played a big role in the ongoing celebration of this art, which has helped increase both its cultural and monetary value.

CHARLES GILLAM: Even though I was already working with Barrister's, nothing gave me exposure like having my art in House of Blues—it made a big difference in making people aware of outsider art. People enjoy the atmosphere, they enjoy the music, and they enjoy the art. House of Blues gave the type of exposure to artists that they never would have gotten otherwise.

ISAAC TIGRETT: I can't even imagine what that collection is worth today. After I put it on the walls in Cambridge, New Orleans, and Los Angeles, all of a sudden you started to see it more and more in museums and art galleries—and then people started buying it for their homes.

There will always be critics who feel that the crossroads of art and bar tabs is worse than a deal with the devil—that a nightclub or restaurant is not the proper setting for works of art—that it's disrespectful, even. But Kahren Arbitman, director of the Cummer Museum of Art and Gardens, in an interview with Sharon Weightman that appeared in the Sunday, June 7, 1998, edition of the Florida Times-Union, offered a more positive view. "I think it's good. If we make art this hallowed stuff that's carried with white cotton gloves, it builds barriers we're now trying to remove."

MICHAEL FEDER: When you go to the Museum of Modern Art they have a café there, right? So it's okay to have a café in a museum, but you can't have a museum in a café? The important things are that it's being treated respectfully and that people can see it, and I think in both cases the answer is yes. It was framed with great sensitivity, with magnificent execution by Andrew Wood, who really deserves the nod for that because he almost single-handedly invented a style of framing for Southern folk art that I've never seen before or after. And did we expose this art to a lot of people? You bet we did. When House of Blues came on the scene there weren't that many places to view this art—you had to go to a museum or you had to go to some stuffy gallery. People are intimidated by galleries, so they would never have seen this stuff. But they saw it when they went out for a night at House of Blues.

ABOVE: Each House of Blues is a living gallery where the curation goes beyond showcasing art and includes food, music, and culture in the experience.

ROY FERDINAND: *DRUG FREE ZONE*

Roy Ferdinand of New Orleans, LA, addressed some of the more uncomfortable issues facing urban America. Precisely drafted in ballpoint pen, delicately colored with pencils and watercolors, and often graphically violent, his drawings chronicled what he called "the black urban warrior myth" that calls to many young African Americans in New Orleans and other cities. Although not a gang member or violent man himself, Ferdinand had an acute eye for the details of gang life and urban violence and often characterized his work as "rap in pictures."

ROLAND KNOX: *STAR*

When kids take part in International House of Blues Foundation's Visual Arts Workshop (one of the Blues Schoolhouse programs), Roland Knox is one of the artists cited to explain one-point perspective. His *Star* is situated in the vanishing point from which all diagonal lines emerge to create the illusion of three-dimensional space. The Atlanta-based artist worked for IBM before entering the world of self-taught art. Like much of his work, *Star* contains no paint at all—just beads and shells methodically glued into place.

RUTH MAE MCCRANE: *LOSE HER LORD*

Ruth Mae McCrane is one of the few formally trained artists represented in House of Blues' Art Collection. A visionary and memory painter, McCrane's *Lose Her Lord*, originally housed at Cambridge and now at House of Blues San Diego, is vibrant and evocative of a dream state—chaotic even while ordered by its own sense of reality. "I dream in color," she explained to the *Houston Chronicle* in October 2002. "That's the way the world is. The world is not drab. I don't know anything about drabness. Even when it rains, you can see the rich greens. When lightning strikes, you can see the beauty." Growing up in a strict Catholic household in the Third Ward of Houston, Texas, McCrane was brought up to think that dancing was a sin. However, she soon became immersed in the gospel music at church. Her world was one in which the juke joint and the church were two sides of the same coin, and both were a place of worship through music. At the time of her death in 2002, former House of Blues Art Collection curator Carole Reed commented to the *Houston Chronicle* that McCrane's paintings reflect the "energy of blues history."

RICHARD BURNSIDE: *KING WITH TWO SNAKES*

"This art—it never existed on this earth till it came out of me," Richard Burnside famously explained of his work. Born in Baltimore, Maryland, but perhaps most familiar with North and South Carolina, Burnside served in the military before claiming to receive a vision in 1980. He would continue to receive visions of ancient kings and queens, religious symbols, and mystical insects and animals (like spiders, snakes, wolves, and cats) for years to come, and they would inspire his works—each an allegory of the faith that connects the artistic landscapes of African American and Native American cultures. "He would press his hands up against his eyes and would get images," Michael Feder explains, before drawing attention to the lines, shapes, and dots around the face of *King with Two Snakes*, which "Burnside calls his Roman alphabet, something he made up." Roman alphabet? Not really, but when he's rendering his visions with acrylic paint, marker, and enamel on plywood, Burnside's got a language all his own.

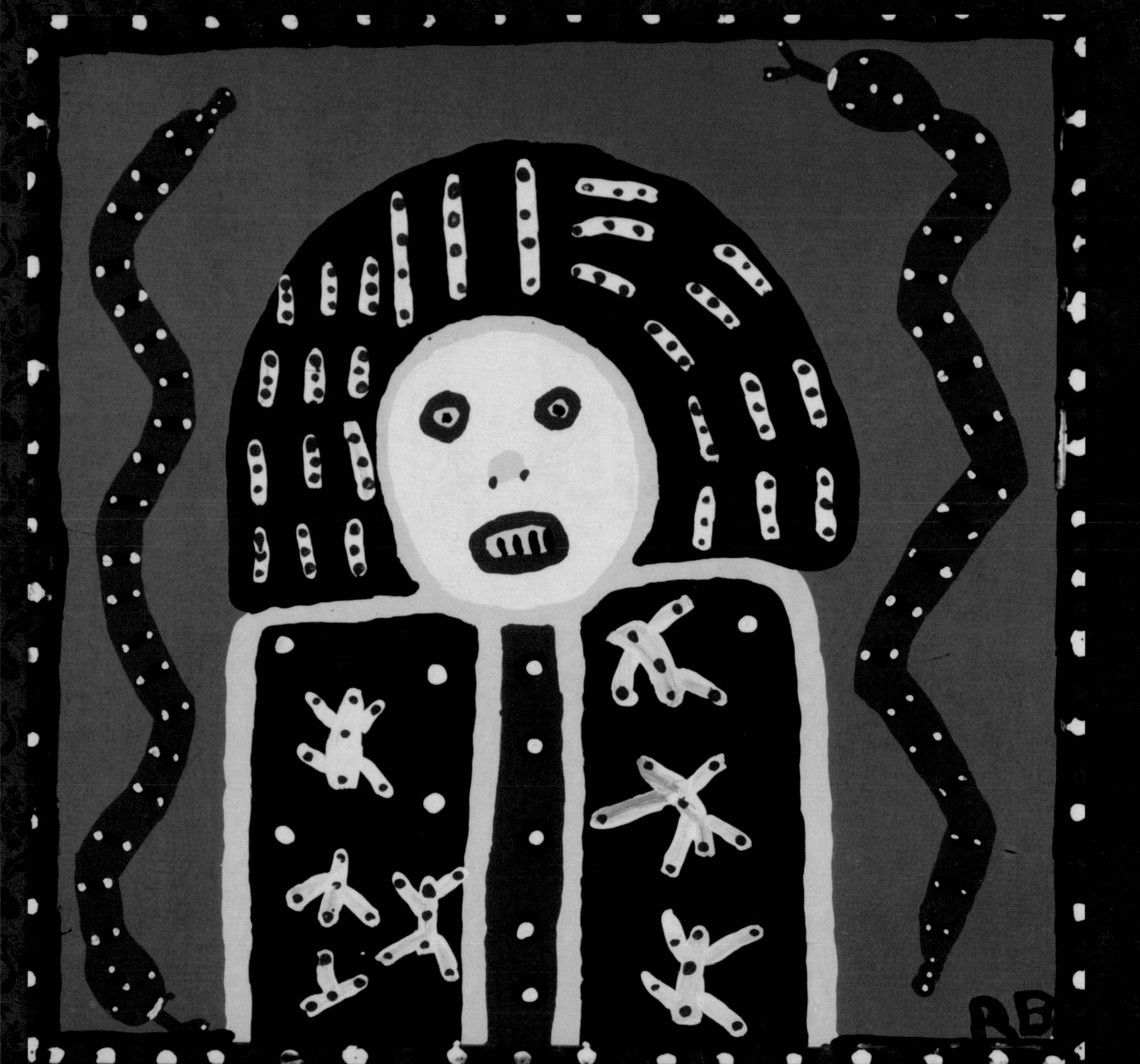
RB

ANDREW WOOD: *BLUES GODS*

Most House of Blues venues feature a special place to pay your respects to the gods of blues and rock and roll—fittingly, these monuments are called *Blues Gods* and were created by English artist Andrew Wood. Creating these was a massive undertaking and required the use of flat photographs as stencils for three-dimensional sculptures, as well as the meticulous creation of a silicone mold for each figure in the sprawling installations. The result is a bas-relief that's a half inch thick and weighs about twenty pounds. Multiply that by 118 and you've got, according to Andrew Wood, one "wildly extravagant ceiling." He elaborates: "The setup costs were phenomenal, and I felt like a medieval craftsman working on a cathedral, completely unknown but doing my service." In the end, the assignment became not only a labor of love but also one of devotion. In his research, Wood became spiritually connected with characters represented in his sculptures. "My engagement with these beautiful and noble faces made it clear that there was a whole other dimension to this work."

LORD GANESHA

Directly above the stage and "Crazy Quilt" curtain is another wall of holy proportions. More laid back than the Western Wall in Jerusalem, and with universal appeal, the "God Wall" *(see page 145)* features many religious symbols representing the globe's most popular faiths, from Judaism and Christianity to Buddhism and Islam, as well as others, such as Native American spirituality, which is represented by the medicine wheel turtle. And just as a Hindu prayer blesses each grand opening, Andrew Wood's *Lord Ganesha* sculpture is a faithful rendition of the deity that removes obstacles and grants success to all who worship him. The Ganesha sculpture is the perfect good luck charm to hang above the stage, not unlike Harlem's "Tree of Hope" at the Apollo Theater. Andrew Wood also created the frame for his *Lord Ganesha*, as he had done for the whole House of Blues Art Collection. He may have felt like the unknown craftsman, but he didn't go unnoticed. "Andrew is a brilliant three-dimensional artist," declares Michael Feder. "He took his sculptural sensibilities to framing and, in essence, created three-dimensional art with frames, which are brilliant works of art in and of themselves."

SCOTT GUION: *HEAVENLY MURALS*

Andrew Wood's *Blues Gods* ceilings may have us looking up to the sky at the deities of blues and rock and roll, but that doesn't make Scott Guion's murals in Boston and Houston any less heavenly. Passersby on Lansdowne Street can see his homage to R. Crumb's *Heroes of the Blues* series on the venue's front doors (featuring Billie Holiday, Sonny Boy Williamson, and Muddy Waters, among others), but inside the club viewers can immerse

themselves in a panoramic landscape that evokes the Mississippi Delta with "Blind" Willie McTell, Memphis Minnie, Lead Belly, and Charley Patton seated on clouds hovering above terrain that evokes the Mississippi River. Diners inside Crossroads at House of Blues in Houston also have one of Guion's sprawling murals to behold. There, the blues gods are Johnny "Guitar" Watson, Big Mama Thornton, Lightnin' Hopkins, and Albert Collins [see pages 70–71]—all are connected to Houston, and each one is given a golden halo right out of a Giotto painting.

ANDREW WOOD: I was very involved in the framing of the folk art, because I have a long history and interest in outsider art. I remember flying in from Los Angeles for the opening of Cambridge, and Isaac took me to this framing company in downtown Boston. I saw that he was about to spend a million dollars on these big corporate-y brass frames. I said, "Hold on, I think we can do this ourselves. It would be cheaper and fit the juke joint message of House of Blues more appropriately." I spent the next week making about one hundred frames, and I invented a style of doing it that I felt was complementary to the work and helped present it in the right way.

In the same Florida Times-Union *piece from 1998, Bill Arnett, one of the nation's renowned private collectors of outsider art, added, "What I hope is that House of Blues will expose people to the art, will generate interest in this art." And patrons do get turned on to the art. A pamphlet about* the contributions of self-taught artists is on every table, and the staff is always eager to enlighten.

In fact, one afternoon in the fall of 1994 Isaac Tigrett gave Mr. Tambourine Man himself, Bob Dylan, a guided tour of the art collection at the Los Angeles House of Blues. "I took him through two hundred pieces, one at a time," Tigrett recalls, "and he asked about every one. I explained where the artists were from and what materials they used." As the doors opened for business and patrons started making their way in for lunch, they were astounded to see Dylan hanging out and viewing the art. Dylan asked Tigrett if he could invite his son, Jakob (of the Wallflowers), to get the tour. "I got three security guards to stand between the crowd and Dylan," Tigrett said, "and he gave his son the tour. He remembered everything I had explained. Then he came to me and said, "This is really far out. Would you mind if I played here?" I told him that it would be an honor. Then Dylan upped the ante, saying, "I do folk art, too. Would you mind if I hung one of my pictures here?"

PAGE 158: Jon Bok installation on display at HOB L.A. **ABOVE:** *Untitled* by Jon Bok. **OPPOSITE TOP:** *Yellow King* is another example of Burnside's somewhat abstract portraiture and use of his "Roman Alphabet." **OPPOSITE BOTTOM:** *Oppression* by Georgia folk artist Archie Byron.

MICHAEL GROZIER: In the early days, we were just goofy enough to greet a customer and say, "Today's special is tomato basil soup, and we're featuring the art of Mose T. See that painting over there? That's Mose T. He paints self-portraits over and over again . . ." Things like that made us different. From the very beginning we were creating a tapestry of what we celebrated. People didn't just leave entertained—they walked away thinking about creativity in a different way. We gave tours in the early days because the art and artists are an important part of who we are and what we are presenting. The art tells a story— everything in our restaurants represents a belief, a passion, or a moral tale. It tells what the artist was seeing and feeling—and that's what the blues is about, too.

More than cool decorations on the walls, House of Blues' Art Collection complements (completes) the juke joint aesthetic, mirroring in its eclectic makeup the pieced-together architecture of every venue—venues where repurposed corrugated tin roofs shelter masterpieces carved from scraps of wood. But even more important than the varied mediums that make up these vernacular expressions are the personalities behind them.

Many of the artists represented by House of Blues are self-taught, and many are visionaries whose work draws from Southern and folk traditions of religion and patriotism, as well as everyday struggles with poverty and constraints on liberty and self-expression. But this framework does not do justice to the staggering scope and diversity of the artists and works showcased by House of Blues.

In a single glance, one might take in works by Roy Ferdinand, a self-proclaimed urban realist whose works focus on the darker side of urban life in his hometown of New Orleans, portraying gun violence, prostitution, drug use, and police brutality in an effort to record an otherwise marginalized history; Jimmy Lee Sudduth, an Alabama-born harmonica player who familiarized himself with thirty-six different shades of mud and painted with his fingers because "fingers don't wear out"; Roger Lee Ivens, also known as Ab the Flagman, who creates endless permutations of the American flag made from scraps of wood and old furniture; and Alyne Harris, a memory and visionary painter from Gainesville, Florida, who derives inspiration from rural landscapes, African American life, and religious themes. And these are just a few of the more than 150 artists House of Blues represents in an effort to exalt this quintessential American art.

International House of Blues Foundation

It's 10 a.m. on a Wednesday morning, on the corner of Sunset and Olive, outside the world-famous House of Blues in West Hollywood. It's an ungodly hour for almost any musician who's accustomed to performing into the wee hours of the night, and especially so for those party people who frequent the Foundation Room. But the show must go on, and while the House of Blues crew is still hard at work breaking down last night's show they've already set the stage for another performance to begin for a very different audience: grade-schoolers. House of Blues is about to be transformed from a world-class concert venue to a multimedia classroom, a literal Blues SchoolHouse.

Weekday mornings during the school year, House of Blues opens its doors to students and teachers attending the Blues SchoolHouse program offered by International House of Blues Foundation (IHOBF), a 501(c)(3) nonprofit organization supported by House of Blues, House of Blues Foundation Room members, and other donors. Created in 1993, IHOBF provides resources and educational programs in the arts for students and teachers in cities where House of Blues venues are located. Hundreds of thousands of students and teachers nationwide have traveled to

a House of Blues to participate in the Blues School-House and other IHOBF programs, which include art tours and workshops related to House of Blues folk art collection; Cultural Journeys drum-based music programs; annual Dr. Martin Luther King Jr. programs; and Action for the Arts student performances, exhibits, and competitions. IHOBF also extends its reach beyond the walls of House of Blues by providing arts education resources for teachers and support for youth arts programs. In 2012, for example, IHOBF's Instruments, Arts Resources, and Grants Program was introduced across the thirteen House of Blues locations and more than $200,000 worth of musical instruments and grants were awarded to school and community-based youth arts instructional programs. Students in these programs get to perform onstage at House of Blues venues.

"Any jazz fans here today?," Meloney Collins, vocalist and co-narrator of the Blues SchoolHouse band, asks the students seated inside the club. Hands rise and students shout out their approval in a chorus of "Yay!" Collins continues, "How about gospel? R&B? Rock and roll? Soul? Funk? Hip-hop?" As she works her way through the musical genres, hands go up and the "Yays!" continue. Maybe they're ecstatic because

---

ABOVE: Blues SchoolHouse in session at HOB L.A. **OPPOSITE BOTTOM:** Students performing during the annual celebration of Dr. Martin Luther King. The Inspired By His Words programs put on by IHOBF highlight Dr. King's commitment to social justice and equality. **OPPOSITE TOP:** IHOBF hosts a number of youth music classes, affording underprivileged youth an opportunity to explore their talents and their cultural connection to music.

they are on a field trip and out of school, or maybe they have cool parents who expose them to a lot of music, because these kids really seem hip to it all.

Collins directs the students' attention to a large screen featuring a diagram of a series of circles arranged around a single circle in the center. The outer circles are labeled with music genres: hip-hop, rock and roll, R&B, gospel, jazz, funk, and soul, each connected by a line to the blues circle in the center. Collins sums it up: "All of these musical forms that I just asked you about were influenced by the blues. It all connects back to the blues." And from that launching pad, the kids in attendance embark on a musical and historical journey, one that chronicles developments in American music and culture along a timeline of historical events, as if their social studies class were combined with their music appreciation class in one completely engaging presentation.

Collins, co-narrator Lamont White, and the full Blues SchoolHouse band are onstage to lead the journey, with the narrators telling the story and the band

bringing it to life with music. The students travel with them to West Africa in the 1500s to learn about African musical traditions and join the band to create polyrhythms and sing in call-and-response style. They then travel from Africa through the Atlantic slave trade over to what is now the United States, where by force Africans were enslaved; under the harsh conditions of slavery they created the music that would eventually become the blues. The journey takes students through field hollers, spirituals, the abolitionist movement, the Civil War, the Emancipation Proclamation, and Jim Crow laws. They experience the early forms of the blues as it evolved alongside the African American narrative of the Great Migration from the rural South of the United States to the big cities of

the North and West, where the blues were amplified and electrified. As the journey continues through the civil rights movement, the tumultuous '60s, and the decades that followed, students experience the influence of the blues on R&B, rock and roll, soul, funk, and hip-hop. Once these dots are connected, it would be hard for these kids to ever forget it, and perhaps they would never listen to music the same way again. At least that's what IHOBF Program Manager Nazanin Fatemian thinks. "I'm always surprised to hear them when they're leaving," she says. "They'll be singing Muddy Waters and Jimi Hendrix on the way out. I'm pleased that that's what they're taking away with them; so much of the Blues SchoolHouse experience is about exposing them to the story of the blues and to musicians who contributed to blues music and related styles." The effects of the program are not only long lasting but often life altering, Fatemian explains. "Many of the students leave inspired by what they've learned and with a new or renewed interest in expressing themselves creatively."

If you think that getting students to hum along to some of yesteryear's music as they exit is just a small side effect, then you may be underestimating the power of music to effect social change. It's all

there in the Blues SchoolHouse playlist: from Marvin Gaye's "What's Going On" to Edwin Starr's "War" to Stevie Wonder's "Living for the City" and Grandmaster Flash's "The Message"—which really brought down the house. The students learn about individuals and movements that brought about social change, and they leave with the message of social responsibility, self-empowerment, and racial harmony.

IHOBF's first executive director, Mark Princi, is a proud believer of not only the program's effectiveness and purpose but also the fundamental need for the program. "America is a place that doesn't have a minister of culture or anything like that, so you get very little art and music training in the schools," he laments. And with budget cuts and limited resources going to art and music programs, despite overwhelming evidence showing that students who receive these benefits do much better in all other areas of school, Princi had nothing but sympathy and support for the teachers who are left to pick up the slack. "They are the real heroes. They would make calls to reserve a day that they could come down, and they would be so delighted to come, but they

didn't even have the money to hire a bus to get the students there, so they would write letters for grants to get the money. They were amazing and helped make the program a really big success."

From the inception of House of Blues, even before there was a Foundation Room (that swanky private club established for the very purpose of funding IHOBF), there was a dual mission to increase the public's awareness of African American contributions to American culture and to enlighten America's youth about the cultural impact of the blues and its vast influence on contemporary music. Says IHOBF Executive Director Susan Jauron, "Isaac Tigrett's vision from the beginning was that House of Blues would serve as an arts and cultural educational resource for youth—a place where students and their teachers could learn about history, culture, and social change through live music and visual art. Isaac recognized the important role that music plays in the lives of young people; he was fond of saying that all young people are musicologists before they grow up and discover mortgages and marriage. Engaging youth with music, and blues music in particular, made perfect sense to him."

So what do these musicologists need to take the music from the nineteenth and twentieth centuries into their present and future? The organization that once put on a Little Richard–hosted web-conferencing session between schools in Los Angeles, Chicago, and Boston is looking to bolster its online resources for schools that want access to IHOBF's programs. Jauron's forecast looks optimistic: "The next phase will be to expand IHOBF's online learning center so that teachers and students everywhere can benefit from the arts and cultural content that has been created over the years." Other plans for the future include increasing grant and musical instrument awards to youth arts programs and creating additional performance and exhibition opportunities for young artists.

It may manifest itself in Blues SchoolHouse programs, musical and visual arts competitions for youth, student performances onstage at House of Blues, artistic tributes to Dr. King, or instruments and grants for schools, but the primary goal of IHOBF—encouraging young people to explore and express their creativity—will never change.

OPPOSITE: In addition to music programs, IHOBF creates opportunities for students to learn about art and hosts a multitude of hands-on workshops. **TOP AND ABOVE:** IHOBF is taking broad strides in fostering the next generation of musicians and musicologists, as well as inspirational orators.

chapter seven

HOUSE OF BLUES LEGACY

House of Blues is a juke joint like no other: It's a roadhouse, it's the devil's fishing pond, it's a house of worship, it's a place where you can lose yourself in the music, it's a moment when you find yourself in a lyric, and it's a venue where you can dance and sing your troubles away—if only for a few hours. That's what House of Blues is all about, and that's what the blues is all about—in its original form and in all of its variations. We sing the blues when we want to remember, and we sing it when we want to forget. We sing the blues because it's an analgesic that numbs the pain, and we go right back to the blues as an intoxicant when we want to celebrate life. But at the end of the day, no matter if it's happy or sad, fast or slow, acoustic or electronic—it's all the blues, and it's all House of Blues.

It's been two decades of letting it all hang out. And if the artwork on display at House of Blues has been described as the visual blues, then the essence of House of Blues itself has also shape-shifted into various incarnations throughout the years. In addition to the thirteen venues, there was also *House of Blues Radio Hour* (now *The Blues Mobile with Elwood Blues*, during which Elwood Blues himself schools you in the blues). Couch potatoes could watch *Live from House of Blues*, which aired to millions every week on TBS and featured musical guests such as Yes, the Psychedelic Furs, Public Enemy, and the Dave Matthews Band. House of Blues took over the television once again when the nation tuned in to Super Bowl XXXI's half-time show, starring the Blues Brothers (with all the backup dancers dressed in matching hats and shades), James Brown, and ZZ Top. When the masses still bought CDs, House of Blues sold many via House of Blues Records, a label so prolific—releasing some highly

coveted theme and tribute albums as well as artist albums by the Derek Trucks Band, Roger Daltrey, the Blind Boys of Alabama, and other world-class artists— that it took blues enthusiast Tom Tourville seventy-four pages to meticulously catalog all 114 releases.

Pop-ups? House of Blues was ahead of that game as well, bringing the party to the Atlanta Summer Olympics. At the games, House of Blues also had an opportunity to show their true character as blues preservationists and put the original Muddy Waters cabin, the one from the Crossroads that Alan Lomax visited so long ago, on display for the world to see. At the same time, the Blues Brothers (Elwood and Zee) were proselytizing the blues to a journalist in France via a cyber chat through House of Blues–sponsored Java Joint Online—and yes, this was happening in 1996! Despite the overwhelming cost and uncertainty that saddled the cyber age, House of Blues put its money where its mouth was and took the blues online.

ABOVE: Muddy Waters's cabin restored and ready for display at the Atlanta Summer Olympics. **OPPOSITE:** Blues musicologist Keb' Mo' performing at HOB L.A. in 2004.

168

DAVE FORTIN: This company had put its cards on the table, and it was going after the digital boom in a really big way by recording concerts and offering them over the web. We were the first company to ever do pay-per-view broadcasts over the web [Ziggy Marley, Chicago, September 1999], and when that all came tumbling down a lot of companies would have folded. I remember a *Daily Variety* issue that read, "House of Blues— The future of live music?" That's how much we had invested in it. We definitely rode some storms. It's a testament to our core business—we put on live music and people want to see live music, and if you do that well, you can ride through some storms.

Nobody can say what will happen at House of Blues during the next twenty years, but a little introspection can be an important step in moving forward with confidence and optimism.

DAVE FORTIN: Reflecting back on twenty years, I'm glad House of Blues didn't expand at the pace that some of the other multilocation companies did. Once there was talk of having a House of Blues in every city in America. I'm glad that didn't happen because I think it allowed us to become a different type of company. After twenty years we only have thirteen venues, and yet people think we have twenty, thirty, forty locations because the brand is so big. People think we've been around for forty years because there's such a historical legacy of music and artists who have performed. That said, I hope the next twenty years does see us expand a little bit more; it's time to get some venues in Europe and other parts of the world. Looking back, I think the company had a lot of lucky breaks: There's been a lot of skilled and talented people holding on to the reins during some tricky times, so to survive with thirteen locations and have a brand as big as it is, is a pretty amazing thing.

MICHAEL GROZIER: I think there's a bunch of locations out there waiting for us: Nashville seems like an obvious one. Toronto would be a great one. Somewhere in New York City would

be great, Coney Island would be awesome, actually almost any borough in New York would be cool. We get approached all the time, because I think that everybody's looking for downtown attractions, anchor tenants. But it's an expensive proposition; we need a lot of square footage, and I've never seen a business that requires more licenses then we do. I mean, we've got milk licenses, tobacco licenses, cabaret licenses, dancing licenses, live-entertainment licenses, recorded-music licenses, and then there's restaurant licensing. It's not like you can just drop one anywhere; you need unique circumstances for it to really work. We're always trying to build a better mousetrap and to be really great at what we do. If you had an okay

OPPOSITE: Willie Nelson performing at HOB Anaheim, January 19, 2011. **ABOVE:** Koko Taylor performing at HOB Cambridge.

171

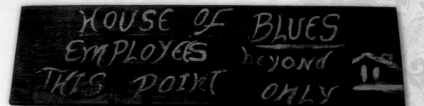

sound system, we're going to have a fucking smoking sound system; if you don't have a nice back stage, we're going to have an amazing back stage. Our intention has always been to figure out how we can do it better, whatever better is today, whatever better is for tomorrow, and whatever better is after that.

DAN AYKROYD: If it were fifteen years ago and we had the money to grow as we wanted to, we could have rolled out Foundation Room clubs separately as Foundation dining establishments, but Live Nation is not interested in primarily being in the restaurant business. It's interested in being a concert venue—one that has good liquor and food sales so that tickets can be subsidized and the consumer can get a good deal. That's what House of Blues is: The food and beverage sales subsidize a fair ticket price, enabling the consumer to come in the door and see a show for a fair price, which enables the band to get paid the dollars that they want to play there. It's a great economic model and one that can work in multiple cities across the world. Hopefully, as the economy turns around and fortunes improve for

many businesses, Live Nation will see that the twenty-year-old establishment known as House of Blues can go anywhere. If it's in a casino in Las Vegas it can go into a casino in Macau, it can go to Monte Carlo, it can go to Paris, London, Toronto, New York City, Miami, and other cities—and hopefully in the next ten years we will see this occur.

DAVE FORTIN: Live Nation came on board and bought us at a very pivotal time, when not only investors who have been with us for a long time can be made whole, but they also take us to a new level. Live Nation has that incredible span of venues around the world whereby you might start at the Parish room in New Orleans, which holds three hundred people, one day and, God willing, you'll be playing a Live Nation–produced show at the Rose Bowl the next.

OPPOSITE: Early new-wave rocker Elvis Costello performing at HOB L.A., February 2004. **ABOVE:** Gavin Rossdale of Bush performing at HOB Anaheim, June 2009.

House of Blues is a place where artists can become stars and where stars can live for their art. It's where fans can rub elbows with pop culture royalty and where rock gods go to be fans again. It's not just the delectable food on the plate, the art on the walls, or even the bands onstage; it's unforgettable experiences, it's a lifetime of memories. There's some elusive realness in the air at every House of Blues—old-timers call it mojo, while others identify it as a culture, and still others simply call it magic.

ISAAC TIGRETT: The legacy of House of Blues is that it did exactly what it was supposed to do: raise the awareness level of blues music as the granddaddy of all American music. It also raised the consciousness of the African American contribution to American society and its arts and music scene. House of Blues became the basic teacher of where American music comes from—its evolution to rhythm and blues to rock to rap—just like the show House of Blues puts on at the school [IHOBF's Blues SchoolHouse]. I'm honored that the good Lord allowed me to represent that culture. I remember all the people who came to House of Blues for the music, but it sometimes seemed more like congregational prayer.

KEVIN MORROW: What a lot of people don't understand is that House of Blues is so great that I almost got it tattooed on my chest! I've never in

my life felt more connected to a company than when I was at House of Blues. It's more than a brand; it's a family. It was easily the most fun that I've ever had. Sure, I've made more money elsewhere, and put on bigger shows, but for the actual vibe, the whole package? I couldn't wait to go to work. It's a blessed life to go to work with all those legends and be there for all those performances. Sometimes my friends back East say, "You get to see shows, you go to openings . . ." and I say, "Oh my God! This is why I'm here!"

SCOTT KAPP, GM HOB Cleveland: Being a part of the House of Blues team means a career of long hours, constant change, and opportunities to see and do things that others only dream of. There are eighteen-hour days that disappear in an instant when you stop to watch John Lee Hooker play guitar on our stage; or weeks of no days off that are all but forgotten when you hoist that pint while sitting in a dark corner of the building with U2. Seeing that band for the first time as an opener, and you just know they are going to make it . . . and a short time later you get to say "I called that one" as they play one of our big rooms and beyond. It's a great feeling when a fan tells you their story and how much House of Blues has meant to them, and in some cases (now after twenty years) are carrying the flame through their children's experiences at House of Blues. Us "old timers" all have incredible memories, stories to share, and most of all a network of friends and colleagues, that, like a secret society, know the handshake and understand without a word what we've been part of and how we've made an impact on the world.

MARK PRINCI: House of Blues was probably the best four years of my life. If House of Blues were a real person, a friend right in front of me that I was toasting, I would say, "I don't know what I did in my lifetime to deserve to be your friend, but if I did know I'd do it again."

ARICH BERGHAMMER: Unless you were a part of it from the inside, it's hard to explain—it's kind of like a band of brothers. We were taken

to extremes, and because of that I've been blessed. I've seen things that I never would have experienced in my life otherwise. I've seen things that most people wouldn't believe. And if the man upstairs tapped me on the shoulder and told me it's time to leave I would be fine with it, because in life I got to stand next to Tupac, John Fogerty, Lauren Hill, and a Beatle [Paul McCartney]. It's been unbelievable.

NIGEL SHANLEY: I always find that word *legacy* weird. I don't think you can get away from the fact that House of Blues *is* Isaac Tigrett—to me that's the legacy. Isaac Tigrett showed the planet how to be a success by giving rather than taking. That's the original idea of House of Blues: that you can make a fortune by giving. It might take you longer, you may not get as much, but how much do we need?

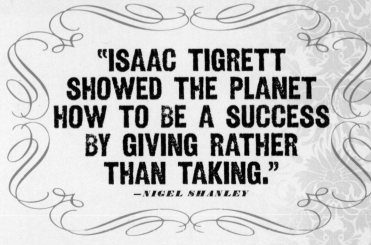

"ISAAC TIGRETT SHOWED THE PLANET HOW TO BE A SUCCESS BY GIVING RATHER THAN TAKING."
—*NIGEL SHANLEY*

ISAAC TIGRETT: Through telling the story of House of Blues I got to relive some of the most precious days of my life. To be associated with all those wonderful kids who work there, to be able to bring joy to so many people. Nothing turned me on like bringing people all that pleasure.

OPPOSITE: Nothing builds anticipation like a piano waiting for the likes of Tony Bennett. HOB L.A., February 2007. **ABOVE:** Flaming Lips always put on an electric, interactive performance, and they feel right at home among the Mardi Gras traditions of New Orleans.

For people like Paul Shaffer, Jim Belushi, Dan Aykroyd, and countless others, House of Blues will always be the home of the Blues Brothers—the duo that went on a mission from God to turn people on to the original blues heroes and to keep the spirit of the blues alive. And just because John Belushi (aka Joliet Jake Blues) isn't physically around to see his triumph, it doesn't mean that his presence isn't felt in every single one of those thirteen locations, particularly every time someone puts on that hat and those shades. House of Blues is still, at the end of the day, the place where the everyman can buy a ticket, walk through the door, and turn into a bona fide Blues Brother. Understandably, other than honoring his brother by playing the role of Zee Blues, Jim Belushi is quite reserved about speaking for his brother, telling us how much he would appreciate the legacy of House of Blues, the place that built a home for the Blues Brothers. Thankfully, Dan Aykroyd (aka Elwood Blues) isn't as reticent.

DAN AYKROYD: We dedicate what we do to John every time we open a House of Blues with a Sacred Hearts band—the voiceover basically says, "Please welcome two men from Calumet City, Illinois, who live to keep the music of their brother Jake alive." And that's what we're all doing. We're there to keep the flame burning. We're there to keep his spirit with us. And so whenever I walk in, I'm always conscious of how much John missed. He missed out on House of Blues. And so I have to live for him and vicariously do the things that he would have done, which makes me enjoy the place all that much more. His brother Jimmy feels the same way. I think that anyone who works there, anyone who comes into the bar and sees John's picture, immediately associates House of Blues with great times and great entertainment, from his work on *Animal House* to *The Blues Brothers* to *SNL*.

His spirit stays alive because of the conscious effort on my part and his brother's part and those who knew and loved him, and that really hits home when we're opening a House of Blues and we get to play. Jimmy and I get to take on the persona of the Blues Brothers and honor John by dedicating our show, the opening of the club, to him. John would have ruled the roost here at House of Blues. I imagine him in a club in Las Vegas, Chicago, New Orleans, and Los Angeles, having these great incredible nightclubs to bring the fans to and him saying, "Hey, I helped build this." He would have related to it big time. He would have just loved it.

JIM BELUSHI: Let the magic ride. This should be an institution like the *Today Show* or *Saturday Night Live*; it should go on for decades. This is the place where magic happens.

ISAAC TIGRETT: For many years promoters would offer dumps for a greenroom to hang out in, old basements with no ventilation and an old Naugahyde sofa to sit on. Musicians would tell me, "They treat us like meat! They say stuff like, 'Change in the car!' and, 'Yes, of course you have to pay for a towel!' and 'Get your gear out of here, already!'" Dan and I believed that we needed to treat the artists like our family, and every House of Blues we built is totally artist oriented. We made beautiful greenrooms with free bars inside; we give the lead guy in the band a limo so he can go anywhere with his wife, and we have lists of other clubs, restaurants, and attractions for the rest of the band and especially their crew. We recognize that the most important people in the band are the lighting crew and the sound cats; bands may come and go, but these guys come back for years. We make sure that when their trucks pull up we help them unload. Everybody is treated like a king—because these are our gods. I want them to be worshipped, with the most beautiful back stage and best service possible.

DAVE FORTIN: I saw that hospitality all the time, especially from Teo. Whether he was going up to the bar and ordering a bunch of food to go so [the musicians] could leave on a full stomach, or reaching into his pocket to give them a little bit extra on behalf of House of Blues, Teo knew what their struggle was like as musicians.

BOOTSY COLLINS: If the world brought people together like House of Blues did, our jobs would not be considered work, because we would be

working just to get off with each other. If we could all learn one thing from House of Blues it would be the power of becoming One, as it should be for fun and the funk of it all. House of Blues has tapped into this in a way, and I am very happy to have experienced it and will continue to experience the joy and self-expression this place allows.

WAYNE KRAMER: The thing that makes House of Blues important for me is the regard with which they treat the musicians. You know from inception Aykroyd and his partners honored musicians, specifically old blues artists. I've played in House of Blues venues across the country, and they are consistently professionally run: They say the sound check is at three o'clock; it's at three o'clock. They say dinner is at four o'clock, and it's at four o'clock. The food is always first rate, and the technical side—the sound, the lights—are

always first rate, and so are the accommodations for the artists; you know they give you a decent room to hang out in with your own toilet! And some have showers! The average person might not think that's a big deal, but if you're living on a bus and going from one gig to the next the next night, then good food, a clean room, and a clean shower is a rare thing—it's like civilization.

ROBBY KRIEGER: There was another place, I can't remember the name, down on Santa Monica and La Cienega that was kind of a blues joint, and that's what I think about when I'm in House of Blues. Jim [Morrison] loved that place—I think Jim would have loved House of Blues; it's definitely his kind of place.

ISAAC TIGRETT: I'm a huge fan of Santana, and one day he was at the club in L.A. and someone said, "Carlos wants to meet you. He can't believe this

ABOVE: Richard Nunez's homage to the late John Belushi and his contributions as Joliet Jake Blues.

place. He's freaking out, he loves it so much." I went out to the porch where he was eating, and he came over to me with tears in his eyes and hugged and kissed me. He said, "This is the greatest thing I've ever seen in my life, I'll never forget this place as long as I live!" He really got it! It was wonderful.

CARLOS SANTANA: I was impressed with the art and the vibe, but at the same time I wanted to know who the owner was, and I found out he's a very spiritual person.

STEVE VAI: It was as if the funky, wealthy, quasi-spiritual elite were reading the palms of the living-on-a-tour-bus-and-playing-shit-holes-around-the-country artist. From an artist's perspective, when the venues were launched it was as if a monolith appeared on the touring circuit. The glorious shacks are very consistent all around the country. An artist can expect a warm, inviting, colorfully bohemian backstage area and fat-sounding stages. You can always expect a great meal served by a very friendly waitress. Whenever I see a House of Blues on my itinerary my heart lights up.

FRANKIE "KASH" WADDY: House of Blues is artist-, musician-, and group-friendly. You can't beat it, man. The venues are perfect: The style is immaculate, the staging is always right.

LIGE CURRY: I told George [Clinton] we could do a whole tour just playing House of Blues as far as I was concerned. What I remember most of all is that we all leave very happy, because it's one of the best places to play for musicians. It's a place where a band like us, not concerned about selling records, can go and play and be respected. The shows are always good, and P-Funk is always geared up to go there because the food is good and we love eating!

JONNY "2 BAGS" WICKERSHAM: After a while we got to know and become friends with a lot of the people who work there. It's like we're part of the regular staff, too!

DAVID HIDALGO JR.: Anaheim House of Blues, you are my home away from home!

KEN JORDAN: The catering on the road is generally bad as a rule of thumb, but whenever we play a House of Blues venue we know we're going to get an awesome dinner!

ABOVE: Jonny "2 Bags" Wickersham isn't the only member of Social Distortion who feels at home at HOB. Mike Ness is getting comfortable backstage and contributing a bit of folk art of his own. **OPPOSITE:** Steve Vai enjoys the fat-sounding stage monitors at HOB almost as much as he enjoys the high-powered fans.

SIZE MATTERS

House of Blues has designed the venues so that there is no bad seat in the house. And what's more, there is often no "pit," so fans can be up close and personal with the artist. Sometimes too personal. But mostly just close enough for that cosmic exchange between artist and audience to go on unobstructed. At House of Blues, the music is so in your face you can almost taste it.

CARLOS SANTANA: Maybe it's no accident that people gravitate to see us in this intimate venue. At House of Blues I feel more connected to the audience, and I'm sure they feel closer to me.

ANJALI RAVAL: Even though it's a small, intimate venue, when you're on that stage and looking out, it feels pretty massive. I've looked into the audience and thought, "That's a lot of people." And yet, the artists can see all the faces of the fans because they're looking down on the audience—and they love it. Justin Timberlake is a perfect example: After he did these crazy big arena tours, he came to us and said, "You know, let me do a couple small, intimate shows." He did two in L.A. and one in Anaheim. Artists do it because it makes them remember where they came from, and they love having that smaller, more humble experience.

MICHAEL FRANTI: There are very few venues that are specifically designed for rock and roll. A lot of music venues were originally designed to be movie theaters where everybody was supposed to look up to the screen, and when they're converted to concert halls you feel like you're really far away from the band. But House of Blues is designed so that everybody in the audience can get close, which helps the crowd get into it too, and that's a good thing.

ARICH BERGHAMMER: When you're at an amphitheater, the closest seat is seventeen feet away, past the barricade. But here the audience is standing less than three feet away and they can see the sweat off of Paul McCartney or Paul Simon's nose.

LONN FRIEND: In the sweaty intimacy of the rooms, the riffs hit you right between the eyes.

BOOTSY COLLINS: Up close and personal is the way I love to funk. Can you imagine being separated by a barrier while you are trying to get some mouth? Not a really good takeoff, and a very rough endeavor for a smooth landing. House of Blues puts the people right there so that you can talk and play to them in their ear hole. And for those that do have virgin ears, they will get knocked up for the very first time!

MICHAEL "KIDD FUNKADELIC" HAMPTON: When I'm that close to the audience I'm able to close my eyes and feel that great energy. Then I'm able to really translate that energy to musical notes.

DAN AYKROYD: There was a deliberate intent on the part of Isaac and the founders of the company and the designers to go back to the spirit of a supper club whereby the floor show was, you know, on the floor. At House of Blues, maybe it's not on the floor, but it's certainly not too far above the floor to feel close to the audience. House of Blues is the first company in decades to bring back the hotel ballrooms or showrooms of the '30s and '40s, places like the Copacabana or 21—the first in decades to actually custom fabricate concert halls for the communal experience that we're talking about.

SCOTT IAN: House of Blues has always been an oasis of sorts when you're out there grinding six nights a week. First-class production and first-class hospitality: There's really not much more a band needs. Thanks for taking care of us over the years.

DJ MUGGS: I always enjoy playing House of Blues venues. First off, you know you're going to get a proper meal, and the greenroom is very green, if you know what I mean. [The venues are] built for the live experience, and no matter where you stand you can see the performance. I've played House of Blues many times, whether it was with Cypress Hill or as a DJ, and I always look forward to it.

MELISSA ETHERIDGE: Thank you for keeping precious the roots of the music that changed the

world and continues to change the world. House of Blues pays tribute to those who [made music] back before you made any money doing it. They did it because it was in their soul. It was Muddy Waters, and Robert Johnson going down to the Crossroads. It was the seedy, dark, racially infused beginning, and House of Blues celebrates it; they put it up as a work of art, they keep it safe, and they provide work for those who are still making that music. It's always an honor to play there.

MICHAEL FRANTI: House of Blues is a living legacy. You walk in there and you feel the vibe of all the great artists that have played there and from all the great art that's on the walls, and it makes you feel like, "Damn, I want to be the best performer I can be tonight." And when you perform there you want to leave your sweat on the same spot that Al Green or

ABOVE: B.B. King taking in the love during his February 2013 performance at HOB Anaheim.

Buddy Guy played. It's a great feeling to be part of that legacy.

SCOTT KIRKLAND: So it's twenty years now? Wow! Well, that is pretty cool because next year is our twenty-year anniversary.

KEN JORDAN: That's right, we're both almost twenty-one, let's have a drink.

SCOTT KIRKLAND: Yeah, in the Foundation Room.

CHALI 2NA: The outlet that House of Blues has been for us has been phenomenal. It's a symbiotic relationship that helped us to spread our vibe in a place that's reputable, a place that's respected enough for all walks of life to come check us out—and not just certain styles of people. Everybody comes through, and I think that is amazing. I'm grateful for that. I would say big ups to House of Blues for being twenty years old, and big ups for Jurassic 5 for being twenty years old right along with you.

DAVE KING: I would like to wish House of Blues a very, very great and happy 20th Anniversary on behalf of Flogging Molly. I would like to thank them for putting up with us all these last few years and also giving us great venues to play and [the opportunity to] meet great people. I wish every club could be like House of Blues, because it really does stand out as a premier venue. I would just like to thank them from the bottom of our hearts, because they've made our lives a hell of a lot easier on the road. We've been on the road now for fifteen years, and you always know what you're going to get at House of Blues.

PAUL SHAFFER: I hope House of Blues goes on forever and that it continues to do its part to ensure that live music never dies.

ABOVE: *Flogging Molly shared the stage with the Blues Brothers and ZZ Top to help HOB celebrate its twenty years of contributions to live music.*

TURNIN' IT OUT

The news vans were everywhere, but even their huge antennas couldn't compete with the sight of the oversize loudspeaker mounted on the Bluesmobile, which was right behind the flashing lights of an official police escort consisting of cop cars, police motorcycles, and even a helicopter. For blocks fans could hear the overhead announcement from Dan Aykroyd's alter ego, Elwood Blues. "Sheriff's department escort!" He began his address on this California-cool night of December 4, 2012. "This is Elwood Blues again in the Bluesmobile, directly behind you! We are only two minutes from House of Blues. I repeat: We are almost to House of Blues. There should be a considerable amount of chaos, paparazzi, and crazed and screaming fans upon our arrival. I mean: We are the Blues Brothers!" He demanded, "If not, arrest everyone!" But Elwood Blues and Zee Blues didn't have to worry about there being a sufficient amount of pandemonium welcoming them to the blue carpet—the crowd was rabid and waiting.

Elwood Blues had every right to expect a media mayhem and fan frenzy at his arrival. This wasn't going to be some fluffy cocktail party—hors d'oeuvres be damned when you've got the Blues Brothers, Flogging Molly, and ZZ Top on the menu. For twenty years this Blues Brother has been banging the House of Blues drum and wearing its heart on his black-suited sleeve, honoring the legends that came before him, supporting the artists who have come into their own on the venues' stages, and tirelessly welcoming the fans who come to see them. Whether for educating listeners about the blues pioneers on *House of Blues Radio Hour* (now *The Blues Mobile with Elwood Blues*), gifting James Brown with gold coins as gratitude for opening new locations, or simply buying a round of drinks and laughing a night away with friends and fans in the Foundation Room, Elwood Blues has left his mark on the scene, and Dan Aykroyd has put some serious time (and money) into his juke joint—and both have earned the right to roll in hot down the Sunset Strip.

ABOVE: Elwood Blues finished his speech with a reminder of what HOB is all about: "We embrace all music and all culture, and we celebrate African American culture, and also Albanian blood."

Twenty Thanksgivings after its humble beginnings in an old Cambridge house, House of Blues began a yearlong party celebrating twenty years of music, memories, education, and a still-blooming drive to give back to the community. House of Blues gave thanks with Feed the Souls, a mission to feed twenty thousand people who otherwise may have gone hungry for the holidays. Las Vegas doubled-down on the spirit of giving when it hosted "Happy Anniversary Hour" during twenty days from November to December, with each day devoted to helping out various charities, from the Leukemia/Lymphoma Society and Toys4Smiles to House of Blues' own International House of Blues Foundation (IHOBF). Additionally, one dollar from every 20th Anniversary Concert Series (featuring Flogging Molly and other acts) sold was donated to IHOBF's Action for the Arts, a program that funds and promotes music and art classes in schools across the country as well as at House of Blues itself.

It's almost expected that a business based on human values and community building would share its success story by giving back. But it's also presumed that they'd throw a hell of an anniversary party—and they did: a yearlong, venue-wide blowout that kicked off that night in December when Elwood and Zee threatened to crash through the doors of the Los Angeles House of Blues as if it were the Dixie Square Mall in suburban Chicago, riding high on the crest of a police escort and a mob of fans as they snaked their way down Sunset Boulevard.

When the Bluesmobile finally pulled up to the corner of Sunset and Olive, Elwood and Zee wasted no time in strutting their stuff on the blue carpet, where Elwood spoke to some members of the press while Zee looked on in stone-faced-yet-comical silence. Elwood may have slipped back into Aykroyd for a minute—though the absolute sincerity in both voices often makes it hard to tell—when he promised *Rolling Stone*'s Dan Hyman that "House of Blues is going to be more vibrant than it has been in the last ten years. We're moving on from the stage of complacency after survival. That's over now. The survival has been established." Zee finally opened

his mouth when he and brother Elwood serenaded the press with just a tease of B.B. King's "My Kind of Blues." "We sound like cats on a fence now," Elwood apologized, "but it'll improve." It did improve once they got inside, but not before Elwood Blues faced the congregation of artists, fans, and House of Blues family and friends and spoke not only on behalf of House of Blues but *as* House of Blues.

"Greetings, everybody. Thank you for appearing here with us at the corner of Sunset and Olive," Aykroyd began. "This was the third House of Blues that we built in the '90s, and now we have thirteen venues across the country. And then, of course, Live Nation, our parent company—parents, in fact—have thirty-eight venues across the country. And what I am most proud of tonight, as we stand here, is the fact that we've got almost three thousand employees working in these industries across America—in our nightclubs. And this last Thanksgiving we fed more than twenty thousand people across the country. So House of Blues is here on Sunset and Olive for the next twenty years and the next twenty thousand concerts."

As he wrapped up his speech, Aykroyd reminded everyone of what House of Blues is all about. "We've had people from all spectrums of music. We embrace all music and all culture, and we celebrate African American culture—and also," he paused, turning to Belushi, "Albanian blood." And then back to the crowd, reacquainting them with Jim's character and connection to the source: "Jake Blues was my partner, this is his brother Zee; he's from Albania. I found him under a rock. He's related to the King, he sure can shake and shimmy and sing the blues, and we're gonna do it inside!" Jim Belushi then flipped an oversize switch and set off what was not only a fireworks display of 4th of July Kiss-concert proportions, but also the first one the Sunset Strip had ever seen. "Unity in diversity, help ever hurt never," Aykroyd said, bringing it back to House of Blues core values and the reoccurring message borrowed from Sathya Sai Baba. "And we're having a blast tonight," he declared, his final words an invite: "Let's go inside and listen to some great, great music!"

ABOVE: Zee Blues took the cue and flipped the switch on the most riotous fireworks display the Strip had ever seen.

As if being led by the Pied Piper of Ottawa, the crowd followed Aykroyd inside the club, where they were treated to the culinary gifts of resident celebrity chef Aarón Sánchez. As part of the celebration, he had been commissioned to update the menu; guests were served newly created dishes during a preshow reception at Crossroads at House of Blues, while the Foundation Room hosted a three-course fine-dining experience. After all the eating was done and the Clean Plate Awards handed out, it was time to turn that mutha out! And that's exactly what the Blues Brothers, Flogging Molly, and ZZ Top did. The music was on fire, the crowd was electric, and the mojo was in the air—Flogging Molly's Dave King was still high, not just from the experience of playing between the Blues Brothers and ZZ Top but also from hanging out with Dan Aykroyd and Billy Bob

Thornton. "It was just surreal. And they were so nice. I remember standing there with Dan and Jim when my wife, Bridget [Bridget Regan, the Flogging Molly fiddle player], came up and introduced herself, and Jim turned around to Dan Aykroyd and goes, 'Who's this?' And it sounded like he was in *The Blues Brothers*! And Dan Aykroyd goes, 'It's Bridget Flogging Molly!' To me it sounded just like Elwood Blues."

Michael Grozier also made sure to invite Nigel "Mr. Foundation Room" Shanley to the party, to pay respect to House of Blues family members past and present. "I think it's amazing," Shanley said of the gesture. "I remember walking in and the first person I saw was Dan. And he grabbed me and said, 'Oh my God! You're eating with us!' It was Dan and Jim. I actually started acting like I was working at House of Blues again because I followed them around and got

ABOVE: HOB stalwarts ZZ Top brought it, beards, shades, hot licks and all, to the 20th Anniversary bash. **OPPOSITE BOTTOM:** Not only does Elwood do the blues; he's also a great hype man. Quick on the mic while giving Billy Gibbons a solid, and still on a mission from God. **OPPOSITE TOP:** "Monster" Mike Welch performing at HOB Cambridge. His performance at the 20th Anniversary party with Elwood brought the party full circle and primed HOB for another twenty years of performances that will look to the future while celebrating the past. **PAGE 190–191:** Mural depicting blues legend Robert Johnson by artist Scott Guion, on display at HOB L.A.

them drinks and escorted them downstairs. On the way down I ran into Arich Berghammer, and he said, 'My God, you're still doing it, aren't you?'"

Shanley remembers another very special guest in the house that night, one whose relationship also goes all the way back to day one, when House of Blues was a small family home with an even smaller stage. "I walked in and there was 'Monster' Mike Welch, and he hadn't changed, except he was a man now and with his wife. Monster Mike was there since Cambridge. I remember being there with his parents when he signed a record contract with House of Blues Records. I was delighted that Live Nation had flown him out with his wife to be a part of this twenty-year celebration."

It shouldn't surprise that the Live Nation person responsible for hooking up with "Monster" Mike Welch was Dave Fortin. After all, he was there during those bitter-cold Boston winter when a practically adolescent Welch made the roof drip in a hot sweat. "I actually got in touch with Mike," Fortin offers. "I said, 'Hey, Mike, it's been twenty years and we want to have you come out to House of Blues." Fortin recalls how Welch's disbelief went something like, "Are you kidding me? Is this for real?" Fortin then made sure to hook up with a music director named Ed Roth to learn some of Welch's songs in anticipation of his arrival. "It was cool because we were going to reunite Welch with Dan Aykroyd for the first time since opening day, since day one. And Dan got up and introduced Mike, and they just jammed—they just tore it up. It was exciting to have him there with his wife, and I know it meant a lot to Mike."

Fortin reflects, "And who would have thought that [this reunion] would happen?"

Twenty years may have come and gone, but for House of Blues Chief Executive Officer Ron Bension, it's still all about the music and the memories: "For two decades House of Blues has been a special home for fans and performers to share musical moments and memories unlike any others," he said. "As we head into our next twenty years and the next twenty thousand performances, we want to make sure we celebrate in the way we know best: Showcasing the greatest music of today and tomorrow." The party resumed the next night and went on the next day after that into the next month and into the new year, when House of Blues spokespeople were still inviting people down for concerts and charity drives.

House of Blues is almost old enough to buy itself a drink at its own Blues Brothers Bar upstairs—almost old enough to buy you a drink. Maybe you'll be there one night when Dan Aykroyd or Elwood Blues will buy you a round and toast to being on a mission from God, toast to a party that's been going for twenty years strong, toast to a party that's just getting started.

You made it. You stood in line, boogied your tail off, and caught the guitar pick from your favorite band. T-shirt in hand, a lifetime of memories and the music still ringing in your ears. This book, and our legacy, is as much about you as it is about us. The fans. The lifeblood of live music. Your energy powers our venues and ignites our artists. Cheers to you and thank you for being the best fans in the world. See you when the curtain opens, we'll be the ones screaming right next to you.

In Music We Trust,
The House of Blues Family

ACKNOWLEDGMENTS

THE AUTHOR would like to thank the good people at Insight Editions, Live Nation, and House of Blues, with a special thanks to Michael Grozier. A huge thanks to Isaac Tigrett and Dan Aykroyd—it was an honor! Much gratitude to Frankie "Kash" Waddy, Lonn Friend, Ken Sharp, and Dale Sherman, as well as all the publicists who I worked with, especially Cary Baker, Carol Kaye, Patti Collins, and April O'Connor. Thanks to Michael Erlewine for the great blues links, Howard Stovall for bringing me to the Crossroads, and Phil Guidry at UCLA for the encouragement. Thanks to Mark Nardone and Chris Meeks, and a big thank you to Mark "Weissguy" Weiss, Mike Appel, and Judith Karfiol. Cheers to all the photographers, artists, and interviewees who helped make this book happen; to my loving family: Mom, Dad, Roob, Rachel, Shimon, and Eyal. And to Leehe, you are my heart, my soul, and my very best friend in the uni.

HOUSE OF BLUES would like to thank the many blues brothers and sisters who have been a part of its family (notably Michael Grozier, Arich Berghammer, Kevin Morrow, Anjali Raval, Dave Fortin, Allison Meyerson, Paul McGuigan, Sonny Schneidau, Jim Mallonee, Sean Striegel, Anthony Nicolaidis, Michael Yerke, Nigel Shanley, Mark Princi, Michael Feder, Andrew Wood), who told the stories and shared their infectious love for HOB. Overwhelming applause to Dan Aykroyd, Jim Belushi, and Paul Shaffer, who gave their time generously . . . and lastly, thanks to Isaac Tigrett for beginning the legacy.

PHOTO CREDITS

© Dan Aykroyd: page 66 (letter insert); © Alex Berliner: pages 15 (bottom left), 115; © Maryanne Bilham: page 133; © Skip Bolen: pages 25, 41 (top), 44, 49, 76, 79 (center), 87 (top), 87 (bottom right), 94, 96, 100, 101 (bottom), 103, 117, 141, 143, 172, 174, 175; © Tom Briglia/FilmMagic: page 78 (left); © April Brown: page 18 (top left); © Jeff Corrigan: pages 64, 139; © Ingrid Hertfelder: pages 2-3, 4-5, 6, 14, 30-31, 48 (top), 88 (top), 91, 105, 118-19, 121, 122, 123 (top left), 123 (bottom right), 124-25, 126, 130 (bottom left), 132, 135, 136, 146, 147 (top), 147 (bottom), 150, 151, 155 (bottom left), 155 (top right), 158, 159 (top), 163 (top), 164, 170 (inset), 182-83, 185, 186, 190-91; © Paul Jonason: pages 70 (left inset), 70-71 (top), 127, 128, 129, 130 (top left), 130 (bottom right), 131 (top), 144 (left), 145 (top), 152, 160-61; © Erik Kabik/Retna: page 59; © Robert Knight: pages 84, 95, 179; © Komposite Imaging: pages 165 (bottom right), 167 (bottom right); © Jeff Kravitz/FilmMagic: pages 7, 34 (top left), 53, 92; © Nicholas LeGris: pages 110-11, 184; © Rich Linton: pages 85 (bottom left), 178 (top left), 178 (top right); © Janet Macoska: page 62; © Robert Matheu: pages 57 (top left), 102; © James Minchin: page 180; © Kathy Ryan: pages 19, 153 (right); © Jim Saley: pages 17, 18 (bottom right), 28 (top left), 28 (bottom right), 29 (top right), 34 (bottom right), 35, 36, 67, 97, 98 (left), 98 (top), 99, 106 (top), 114 (top), 171, 189 (top); © Will Sample: page 89; © Karen Sanders: page 51 (top right); © Dan Seibold: pages 61 (bottom right), 83, 87 (bottom left), 90, 170, 181; © Studio of Andrew Ryan Shepherd (andrewryanshepherd.com): pages 68-69; © Steve Schwartz: page 82 (bottom left); © Abby Sink: page 54; © Daniel Siwek: pages 78 (top right), 82 (center), 82 (bottom right), 85 (top left), 85 (top right), 85 (photo inserts), 101 (top), 104 (top); © Trish Tokar: pages 8, 10-11, 33, 46-47, 72-73, 75, 86, 108, 169; © Dario Preger: page 42 (top); © House of Blues Archive: pages 15 (top right), 21, 24, 26, 27, 29 (left), 37, 38, 43, 45, 50, 51 (bottom left), 55, 56, 57 (top right), 58, 60, 63, 65, 66, 71 (right inset), 77, 112, 113, 114 (bottom right), 116, 120, 123 (Kirk Franklin and Gospel Brunch cuisine images), 131 (bottom left), 138, 140, 144 (right), 145 (bottom right), 148, 149, 154, 156, 157, 159, 162, 163 (bottom), 165 (top right), 166, 167 (top), 168, 173, 177, 187, 188, 189 (bottom), all posters and insert items with the exception of the letter on page 66 and the photo inserts on page 85.

COLOPHON

PUBLISHER—Raoul Goff

CO-PUBLISHER—Michael Madden

ART DIRECTOR—Chrissy Kwasnik

DESIGNER—Jon Glick

ACQUIRING EDITOR—Steve Jones

ASSOCIATE EDITOR—Dustin Jones

PRODUCTION EDITOR—Rachel Anderson

PRODUCTION MANAGER—Jane Chinn